What if
Tomorrow
Never Comes?

Neil David Schwartz

ISBN: 1484900359
ISBN 13: 9781484900352
Library of Congress Control Number: 2013909219
CreateSpace Independent Publishing Platform
North Charleston, South Carolina
www.whatiftomorrownevercomes.com

THIS BOOK IS IN MEMORY OF
JOANNE HANDELSMAN SCHWARTZ
AND
AMY BETH SCHWARTZ,
WOMEN OF VALOR,
WHOSE MEMORIES LIVE ON THROUGH THE LIVES
THEY TOUCHED

CONTENTS

ACKNOWLEDGMENTS

※━●●━※

There are countless individuals I would like to thank for supporting me with love and comfort during the period in my life when I needed it most.[1] All of the beautiful souls who were there for me are too numerous to list, but here are some of them: Scott Schwartz, Randy and Nancy Schwartz, Dan and Leslie Sackheim, Mike Bluestein, Dr. Jeff and Paula Cantor, Joel and Mary Handelsman, Monique Blum, Rabbi Jerry Cutler, Alan and Nancy Epstein, Dr. George Fischman, Jan and Beth Goren, Rudy Grob, Elisa Johns, Michelle Kaplan, Rabbi Nachi Klein, Larry Kligman, Lenny and Sandy Kligman, Drew Kroner, Debbie and Marty Lewin, Lara Martin, Sandy McGill, David and Monica Mohilef, Barry and Cathy Pearlman, Saul and Sara Pearlman, Joe Penner, Joe Port, Steve and Phyllis Port, Cantor Avrum and Miriam Schwartz, Steve and Gail Shapiro, Arthur and Lee Shaw, Steve and Roberta Wax, Dr. Michael and Janice Weitz, the Abraham Joshua Heschel Day School community of Northridge, and Pressman Academy. Finally, to Nancy, for giving me life's greatest blessing: her love and kindness.

---

[1]   Please note that certain names have been changed in the story that follows.

The Café

April 17, 2012—8:00 a.m.: A typical day begins. I arrive at my office on Ventura Boulevard in Encino, California. I ascend from a subterranean parking structure via elevator. My destination is the eighteenth floor. Upon entering the office, I observe my desk, decorated by the clutter of the unfinished toil from the previous day. My thumb clumsily searches for the computer's start button. I will soon be linked to the Internet highway, communicating with people I may never see. My hand hovers over the mouse as my foggy mind tells me I need my morning coffee.

Slowly I head back to the elevator, descending to the lobby and street. From there I walk about one hundred yards to the café where each morning I make my habitual stop. There, an effervescent young Central American woman welcomes me with a smile. "Good morning, Señor Neil. The usual?" "Si, por favor." "Your Español is getting so good," she says with a flirtatious but factitious wink.

As I wait for my coffee, I see a dark-haired young woman, slender with a touch of sorrow in her brown eyes. She reminds me of someone from my past. I study her face while the barista calls out, "Amy, nonfat latte."

I am overcome by emotion. The bridges we crossed together have now disappeared. Our tomorrows have all melted away. There is no return. *Move forward*, I tell myself. *Move ahead*. The pain is pointed. I blink, and the young lady disappears. Once again I am reminded of the struggle to escape what has become my past.

This was not the start that I had planned for my story, but then I didn't plan on this encounter. There was much that was not part of my design, that I didn't foresee, and that I didn't imagine. We make our choices. We build our lives. We plan for the future. But forces beyond our control can unexpectedly rewrite the script.

Galut

T hey say life is what passes you by when you're busy doing other things. As the window of the world begins to close, we take inventory of what we experienced and what we neglected to experience. We recall our achievements as well as our failures. We endlessly chase elusive dreams as love slips into darkness. Words are the currency of consciousness, yet we have difficulty finding the right ones. Our eyes are the window to our souls, yet we can't make eye contact. The key to my past is now firmly locked and bolted behind closed doors, inaccessible and beyond the reach of even Houdini the magical locksmith. I am paralyzed by the smothering grip of *galut*.

Galut is the Hebrew word for exile. It is more commonly associated with the wandering Jew living in host countries, victim of political, national, religious, or ethnic discrimination. *Galut* can be experienced on another level, spiritual *galut*. Spiritual *galut* occurs when a person is out of sync with his or her soul and struggles to make sense out of a seemingly incomprehensible existence. *Galut* divests you of your dreams, your hopes, your ability to love and be loved. *Galut* crushes and destroys the human spirit.

Being in *galut* is painful. I personally know its strangling hold. Its rolling fog has impaired the lens of my life. *Galut* has robbed me of who I was. *Galut* has emptied my dream bank and poured water on the flame of hope. Yes, I have been to *galut*.

On July 17, 2011, my twenty-seven-year-old daughter, Amy, succumbed to lung cancer after a courageous fourteen-month battle. Approximately three months before my daughter's passing, my wife of thirty-two years and best friend, Joanne, suddenly and unexpectedly died, leaving me as the caregiver for my daughter during the last months of her life.

As I commenced upon a treacherous journey starting on Memorial Day weekend of 2010, at which time Amy was first diagnosed, my life took a detour on a narrow and fragile bridge with the realization that the next step might be the last. I called out to G-d and was answered with silence. I put my hope in modern science and the medical community; they offered no answers. My soul was broken. Where would I get the strength to continue the journey? My answer came in the form of portraits of souls in crisis, some of whom survived their spiritual crises and grew and became an inspiration for me and some who were unable to escape the relentless chokehold of *galut*. The following are portraits of souls in crisis and my mind prints from *galut*.

My Paternal Grandparents

As I look back, I have very few memories of my paternal grandparents. Nonetheless, there are enough memories to paint my first portraits of souls in crisis. Ziggy died when I was about eight years old and Sadie when I was eleven. Ziggy was known as "Pop," and Sadie was known as "Nanny." I barely knew them. I recall seeing Pop on a couple of occasions. He lived in Tucson, Arizona. I never saw Nanny and Pop together. I found out as an adult that they were divorced, a family secret guarded from the tender minds of the children.

Ziggy and Sadie came from Poland, and their marriage was a *shidduch* (Yiddish for an arranged marriage). Their union was worse than a mismatch; it was a disaster. After they wed, they fled the anti-Semitism and difficult life in Poland for the United States. They initially settled in New York, where my father and his older brother, Murray, were born. Pop, according to my father, did well selling paint. He had two paint stores, and the family was comfortable. My grandmother had sisters and brothers living in New York who created a large extended family for my father and his older brother, who was two years older than my father.

Things changed in my father's life when he turned fourteen. Pop had developed asthma and was told by his doctor that he needed a warm climate. The choices were Arizona or California. My grandmother had a childhood friend who had settled in Tucson, Arizona, with her adult son. This sealed the deal. The year was 1936, and the Schwartz family was off to Arizona. My grandfather soon started working as a building contractor. Despite his ease for making money, Ziggy's life was in turmoil. His consumption of alcohol was out of control and hijacked possession of his soul.

Tucson was a tough place for Jews to live in the 1930s and 1940s. My father was subjected to verbal assaults and occasional physical beatings. Soon after they had settled in Tucson, my grandmother's childhood friend moved to San Francisco; her son unexpectedly received a job transfer. My grandmother, a deeply religious and observant Jew, was now isolated from her family and friends and growing further apart from her alcoholic husband. No friends, a barren desert populated by cowboys and Native Americans—this was clearly not the stage desired by Sadie on which to live out her life. I can only imagine how difficult it was for her, an observant Jew whose primary language was Yiddish, isolated and alone in a desert town in the Great American Southwest. Poland and New York were now merely memories.

I remember my grandfather Ziggy as a short, stocky man sporting a Southwest turquoise bolo tie. Gold wire-rimmed glasses framed his face, which was weather-beaten and tanned. He wore an oversized white cowboy hat and brown cowboy boots. He clearly could be mistaken for a Native American. On the few occasions I saw Ziggy, I asked myself, *Is this guy really my grandfather?* He may have looked like a cowboy, but he sure didn't sound like one. He sounded like a character auditioning for the Mel Brooks movie *Blazing Saddles*. On his occasional visits, he would greet me in Yiddish with *"Vuhs mahsta, boytshik?"* ("What's new, little boy?")

Once, Ziggy drove to our house from Arizona in his gray Ford pickup truck. He brought a Stanford University sweater as a gift for me. I was about seven years old; I had never heard of Stanford University. The only Stanford I was familiar with was Stanford Shapiro, who was a friend of my dad's. As he spoke to me, Ziggy omitted a medicated type of odor from his breath. I later associated the smell with my first shot of whiskey. *"Boychek,"* he said, "one day you'll go to Stanford University. And then you will go to medical school and become a doctor. You'll make lots of money, you'll be a *gonsa macher* (big shot) in the community, and you will do the great mitzvah of healing the sick. *A la vai* (it should be)," he said with an affirmative nod of his head. I never attended Stanford University. I never went to medical school. And I never saw Ziggy again.

In 1943, my Uncle Murray graduated from the University of Arizona Law School and took a trip to Southern California, where he fell in love with the Pacific Ocean, Santa Monica, and Venice

Beach. That was it. He decided to pack his bags and came west to practice law in Santa Monica. After visiting him, my father concluded that the beaches and rolling hills of Southern California offered a lot more than Tucson. He finished his studies at the University of Arizona, served briefly in the United States Army, and enrolled at the University of Southern California School of Law.

Our family roots in Los Angeles were now planted. However, the course of our family history was almost altered prior to Dad's move to Los Angeles. After college and before his move, he enlisted in the US Army. While he was in basic training, a gas mask malfunctioned and exploded in his face. Overcome by gas fumes, he lost consciousness. Upon awakening, he found himself in a hospital bed, blind and breathing with the assistance of an oxygen mask. He had pneumonia and was listed in critical condition. My grandparents were contacted and told his prognosis was grim. Ziggy immediately traveled by train from Arizona to Arkansas to be at his son's bedside. Miraculously, Dad survived and regained his eyesight. He also received a medical discharge from the service. Shortly thereafter, he learned that his unit had shipped off to combat, where they all tragically died at the Battle of the Bulge.

After arriving in Los Angeles in 1944, my dad was set up with a dark-haired, brown-eyed, beautiful eighteen-year-old by the name of Arline Gelb. Theirs was love at first sight, and they were married in 1945.

Back in Tucson, Sadie made it official, divorcing Ziggy and following her sons to Southern California. She rented an apartment in Venice Beach. The Venice apartment was very small with a repugnant odor; maybe it was because of the musty smell of the old building mixed with the ocean air and the pot of chicken soup that was always boiling on the stove. The soup had a thick layer of fat floating on top. Within a few minutes of our arriving at my grandmother's apartment, she would offer me a bowl of this most unappealing soup accompanied by the words "*es, boychek, es*" ("eat, little boy, eat").

Looking back at this culinary nightmare, I wonder if maybe it was the chicken soup that destroyed my grandparents' marriage, or maybe it was the chicken soup that turned Ziggy into an alcoholic. Upon further retrospect, I wonder if the toxic soup contributed to the early death of my father from atherosclerotic heart disease.

After I had been forced into having one spoonful of soup and trying not to gag, Sadie would take out two Hershey chocolate bars, one for her and one for me. As we each took a bite of the chocolate, experiencing the bitter sweetness painting our palates, this gravely depressed woman broke into a smile. This was clearly her drug of choice. And with each Sunday visit, as my grandmother grew fatter and fatter, it was evident that chocolate now constituted the staple of her diet.

When my grandmother was not serving soup or Hershey bars, she was crying and screaming, "*No gutnik, mamzer, schikker*" ("No-good bastard, drunk"). This was her barrage of verbal assaults against my grandfather. Sadie was forced to become a stranger in a strange land. Her life as a child in Eastern Europe was behind her. Notwithstanding the brutal, overt anti-Semitism in Poland, she had one of life's greatest blessings there: a loving and supportive family.

Sadie's father (my great-grandfather) was known in Poland as a learned rabbi and renowned *maggid* (storyteller). My father would frequently speak with high esteem of the grandfather he never knew. However, I later discovered the revelation of another family secret. It turns out that my great-grandfather Rabbi Glaser fled the community he served under a cloud of controversy. He was married to his first wife for several years. It was, once again, an arranged marriage, but the couple was incompatible. They were unable to procreate, and no children were born of the union.

Rabbi Glaser then divorced his first wife and eventually fell in love with a much younger woman twenty years his junior. The couple had to flee town after they wed. Perhaps expulsion would be a more appropriate description of what went down. This certainly gives rise to the theory that my great-grandfather fell in love before he was divorced from his first wife. Anyway, I have more than enough problems in my own life, so I will pass on trying to figure that one out.

The couple traveled across Poland, where my great-grandfather reinvented himself in a distant town. Once again, he assumed the role of a popular local rabbi and storyteller. With his young bride, my great-grandmother, he had eight children; the first was my grandmother Sadie.

Like Ziggy, Sadie was short. She had an ever-expanding waistline and a boxy build. Her hair was dark and oily, her skin pale, and her eyes green. She was seriously in need of a makeover. Looking at this unkempt, rotund woman, I could capture in her beautiful green eyes the trace of a once-attractive young woman whose youthful beauty and dreams had now dissipated into a life of darkness and despair.

My father's brother, Murray, would usually join us for the Sunday visits to the Venice Beach apartment. My father was five feet, eight inches tall with broad shoulders and a husky build. He had dark, curly hair and green eyes. Murray was also about five feet, eight inches tall and stocky with green eyes but had light brown hair and a ruddy complexion. Murray was a bodybuilder and very health-conscious long before it became fashionable. He would bring a juicer and raw carrots with him to the Sunday beach visits and offered me a carrot juice chaser after the fatty chicken soup. This was, for a five- year-old boy, a gastronomic nightmare.

Murray seemed to be nice enough. He had a never-ending grin on his face. He seemed to always be in a great mood. However, there were strange and uncomfortable moments with Murray. I call them the drive-by drop-offs. Murray would show up at our house unexpectedly on Sunday evenings at about dinnertime. He would ring the doorbell and, once the door was open, quickly escort my grandmother into the hallway, at which time he would do an about-face, dart out of the house, and slam the door behind him. Moments later, you could hear Murray pealing out with his pedal to the metal.

Sadie would stand frozen in our front hallway, her face couched in a mask of depression and despair. She'd begin weeping with an undercurrent of groaning. My mother would walk in, greet Sadie, and offer her dinner. There'd be no response other than escalated weeping. My mother would then flee to her bedroom and shut the door. Now she was also crying. My dad would walk in after a short hiatus in the bathroom, saying, "Hi, Mom, when did you get here?" There'd be no verbal response—only crying. My dad would ask, "What's wrong, Mom?" "Everything," she would reply.

"Would you like Arline to give you something to eat?" "No," she'd say, continuing to sob. My mother would then re-emerge from the bedroom, visually shaken. "Take her home," she'd say. "I can't stand it." And so my dad would put on his jacket and drive Sadie home. This was an almost weekly occurrence. I wondered if all grandmothers were depressed. Thinking it over in a rare moment of childhood brilliance, I concluded that I was wrong. My other grandmother never cried; in fact, she was always smiling. All grandmothers aren't depressed. It must have been Sadie's chicken soup.

Eventually my mother told Dad that he better tell Murray to stop the drive-by drop-offs. I don't know what happened, but somehow Sadie wound up back in Tucson. Murray, seemingly suffocated by his mother's presence, cut a deal with Ziggy. Sadie and Ziggy remarried. Mom said the reconciliation was orchestrated by Murray. Ziggy had experienced financial setbacks, and spousal support was further bleeding him. Murray convinced him that eliminating alimony would help him financially as well as restore some normalcy to the lives of his sons. As one would imagine, the second marriage was short-lived, and another divorce ensued after a few months, leaving Sadie on a train headed back to Venice Beach.

About a year after Sadie's move back to Venice, she was diagnosed with advanced diabetes. It wasn't long before she became insulin-dependent. However, she refused to take her medication, continued eating Hershey chocolate bars, and spiraled into a deeper and irreversible depression. By then I refused to make the Sunday visits. Little did I know that soon there would be no more Sunday visits to the beach. Sadie had a debilitating stroke. She survived but wound up living the remainder of her life bouncing from different convalescent and assisted-living facilities.

As for Ziggy, I later learned that he met another woman and moved to Phoenix to live with her. After a short period of time they broke up, and Ziggy moved back to Tucson. My dad would talk to him occasionally but not about him.

Around this time, my dad and Murray stopped talking. I didn't know what happened. My mother, on occasion, would refer to Murray as not a nice person. What was I missing? The smiley guy with the juicer and fresh carrots was bad? He was always nothing less than nice to me. He treated my grandmother kindly when he wasn't engaged in drive-by drop-offs. Today, after thirty years as a trial lawyer cross-examining thousands of people, I've learned to look beyond nice smiles. While still appreciating a good smile, I have found that eyes are more important; they are indeed the windows to one's soul.

My father and Murray reconciled when I was about twelve years old. Their estrangement appeared to have been fueled by a combination of my mother's adverse feelings toward Murray, coupled with the fact that if my father never initiated a call to his brother, there never would have been a relationship.

Ziggy and Sadie were now both dead. Sadie died in a convalescent hospital in Los Angeles and Ziggy in Tucson, Arizona. I'll never forget how the death of my grandparents affected my dad. A once-carefree, happy-go-lucky, ambitious young attorney, he now began to turn inward. Nighttime TV became replaced by quiet reading. Much to my mother's dismay, stacks of books would clutter the nightstand adjacent to my father's bed, a habit I assumed, much to my wife, Joanne's, dismay. In that stack of books my father would tell me you could find the secrets to the mystery of life, keys to happiness, and a more meaningful existence. He was desperately trying to find what his parents could never find.

The books were an eclectic collection ranging from *Wisdom of the Fathers* to the writings of Confucius, and while the repertoire would frequently change, *Wisdom of the Fathers* was an anchor, always there and often read. Along with the great Jewish philosophers, the nightstand was inhabited by Confucius and Buddha and also Socrates and Aristotle.

My father escaped the *galut* that encapsulated the life of his parents. He looked within and he studied holy writings, using multiple pathways in his quest to find inner strength and peace. Unlike his parents, he discovered that which he was seeking: peace of mind and purpose in life.

When I was around twelve or thirteen, the Sunday trips returned, but this time Dad and I, along with my younger brother, Randy, would visit Uncle Murray. Just as my mother refused to visit Sadie, she also refused to see Murray. Murray was still smiling and now had a giant sheep dog named Lucky. This dog was big enough to put a saddle on and ride around the neighborhood. Murray had a wife named Sophie. While he was Uncle Murray, she was just Sophie. She was an overly formal, intellectual type. Like Murray, she was also a lawyer. She was clearly on the cold side. She was tall and somewhat manly in her mannerisms. Neither the juicer nor weightlifting equipment appeared to be part of Murray's lifestyle anymore. A protruding stomach had now replaced his once-muscular abs.

My dad and Murray would engage in small talk for about an hour, and the visit would end. He seemed like such a nice guy. Why did my mother dislike him? I approached my mother on the subject, and she once again, without elaborating, simply said he wasn't a nice guy.

Sophie, it turned out, was Murray's second wife. The story began to unfold through the lips of my mother, and she eventually related all of it. My mom described Murray's first wife as an attractive and lovely woman whom she liked quite a bit.

Wife number one wasn't happy about Murray spending more time with his mother than his young bride. She gave birth to a daughter, a cousin I never knew. Murray was so consumed with his mother that he almost missed the birth of his child, and he rarely saw her thereafter. Understandably upset, his first wife moved out with the infant. Murray was so angered that when his wife filed for divorce, he refused to pay child support. He also refused to see his daughter. A short while later, Murray's first wife met and married another man. Murray continued to fail to pay child support and refused to see his daughter. He eventually agreed that the new husband could adopt the child. This released Murray of his child-support obligations but not from carrying a monkey on his back for the rest of his life. Ironically, Murray and Sophie tried to get pregnant for many years, with no success. They went to the top fertility specialist in Los Angeles but to no avail. Murray and Sophie were eventually able to adopt a son.

Many years later, my father's relentless curiosity got the best of him, and he searched for Murray's daughter. My father obtained access to records that revealed the adoption-proceeding documents, including the adopted father's identity. My father at the time was a Los Angeles County superior court judge, and, ironically, his niece's adopted father was also a judge. He was an acquaintance of my father. They actually met many years before as adversaries in the courtroom as young attorneys. My father contacted his estranged niece's adopted father. They chatted, and my dad asked to meet his niece. The suggestion was soundly rejected by the adopted father. He explained that Murray's daughter had no clue that she was adopted and thought that the judge was her natural father. She has had a stellar life full of happiness, and to reveal this potentially traumatic history would undermine the strong foundation upon which she walked. My father agreed and never broached the subject again. However, he did reveal the story to our family in confidence.

When my father told us the name of the judge, my brother and I were shocked. We had both appeared before him on more than one occasion in our capacity as attorneys. We had both had similar experiences. I recall distinctly, although it was many years ago, that upon obtaining a disposition from the bench, the judge asked to see me in his chambers. Perplexed, I could only contemplate the worst-case scenario. I hadn't engaged in any improper conduct; the proceeding was as civil and amicable as a judicial hearing could be. Why did the judge want to see me in his chambers?

Upon entering the judge's chambers, I was greeted with a warm smile and asked to sit down and make myself comfortable. The judge seemed to just stare at me for what seemed like minutes but was probably merely seconds. He then asked if I was related to Judge S.S. Schwartz. I proudly responded, "He's my father." The judge then said, "We had a case many, many years ago when we were both young lawyers. I remember him well. He was a gentleman and a good lawyer." I thought to myself, *At least we're off to a good start.* He asked how my father was doing, and I responded that, aside from some heart-related problems, he was getting along just fine.

The judge then said, "Didn't your father also have a brother, Murray, who was a lawyer?" Once again, I responded in the affirmative and asked the judge, "Do you know Murray also?" "I had dealings with him many, many years ago." The smile disappeared from his face. "How is Murray?" he asked. "Truthfully," I said, "I haven't seen him in years. My father and Murray aren't very close." "That's too bad," he said. "That happens too often in families. Well, it's always nice to meet the next generation of barristers, Counsel. I look forward to seeing you in my courtroom again one day." He stood up and gave me a warm smile and a strong handshake. As I exited his chambers, I almost felt a connection to him. About a year later, my brother Randy related a similar encounter with the judge. Both of these occurred prior to our knowledge that he was sort of part of our family.

The judge retired from the bench a few years ago, and, shortly before his retirement, I appeared before him one last time. This time there was no chamber visit. He was looking somewhat frail. When I announced my name, he stared again for what appeared to be a prolonged period of time. Our eyes locked, both of us knowing that we shared a secret—a secret that, for better or worse, would never be revealed.

What became of Ziggy? While I knew that Sadie died from diabetes and a series of strokes, I fortuitously discovered the shocking and disturbing circumstances of Ziggy's death. The year was 1970, and I was a twenty-year-old student attending the University of Arizona at Tucson. The tapestry of the time was the American counterculture. Most of us were seeking greater meaning in our lives, manifested in spiritual journeys or social activism. I, too, was trying to find myself and define who I was. In that context, I was fortunate to have two wonderful teachers, Rabbi Bob Saks at the University of Arizona Hillel Foundation and Rabbi Moshe Poupko, a recent Philadelphia transplant who served as the rabbi of a tiny Orthodox Congregation Young Israel.

Young Israel was located in a small building, which had previously been a residential home. I'm not sure how they got around zoning restrictions, but somehow they apparently did. I occasionally attended classes at Young Israel with Rabbi Poupko. He looked about ten years older than me. He wore a black fedora; his face was framed with a scraggly black beard and thick eyeglasses. He had moved from Philadelphia to Tucson so that his wife could work on a PhD at the university. He was enthusiastic about reaching out to university students and making the study of the holy writings of our tradition accessible. The rabbi was an insightful teacher who helped me jumpstart my lifelong spiritual journey.

One late afternoon, I arrived early for our class. I observed the *shammas* cleaning the sanctuary.

The sanctuary was actually a diminutive chapel with very limited seating. The *shammas* worked slowly, pushing a vacuum cleaner back and forth. A *shammas* is defined by some as a temple custodian. In Yiddish literature, the temple *shammas* is sometimes portrayed as a clandestine wise man or holy, hidden saint. This poor gentleman lacked the mystique of awe. He was short, balding, wore a black *kippah* (head covering), and his pants were so baggy they appeared to be in danger of falling off his skinny frame. One couldn't help but notice the liver spots on his face, a byproduct of age and years of exposure to the baking desert sun. The *shammas* never smiled and avoided eye contact with me. He seemed more than unhappy, perhaps a ten with a bullet on the miserable scale.

As I studied the face of the *shammas*, the thought entered my mind that this old guy might have known my grandfather. And so nervously I asked, "How long have you lived in Tucson?" He looked at me in disgust. "Why do you ask that question?" For the first time I noticed that the *shammas* was missing most of his teeth. He then started talking to himself in Yiddish, none of which I understood. Finally, after a pause, he responded, "The nineteen forties I came to this *farshtinkener* (stinking) place." "Did you know a Ziggy Schwartz?" The *shammas* seemed to draw a blank. "His real name was Sigmund." "Oh, Sigmund Schwartz, the *shikker*! Of course. He was on the board of directors of Anshi Israel *shuel* (temple). He was a successful building contractor but the biggest *shikker* I ever saw. He outdrank the local cowboys in town.

He eventually killed himself." Chills ran down my spine. I heard more than I wanted to know. The *shammas* then asked, "What does a nice young man like you know of Sigmund Schwartz?" Both traumatized and embarrassed, I responded, "Just a distant relative, a very distant relative." The *shammas* shook his head and said, "You don't want to turn out like him. Oy, vey," he said, closing his eyes.

Upon returning home to Los Angeles for winter break, uncomfortable with discussing my grandfather's death with my dad, I broached the subject with my mother. She responded that Ziggy had developed serious heart-related problems. He was hospitalized, given a poor prognosis, and told to alter his lifestyle. This meant an end to the booze. Ziggy grew despondent. Today, he would have been treated with angioplasty or bypass surgery, treatment modalities not available at that time. So, as far as Ziggy was concerned, his life was over. At sixty-four years old, he went into the bathroom of his small house in Tucson, pointed a .38-caliber revolver to his temple, and pulled the trigger on his life. He never had another drink nor did he ever again witness the breathtaking beauty of another Sabino Canyon sunrise.

Tragically, the pain of an empty life was too unbearable for the grandfather I never knew. And so it ended far from his birthplace in Poland, alone in the *galut* of the desert of the great American Southwest.

My Maternal Grandparents

Actually, their names were not Bertha and Armin until they arrived at Ellis Island. Like it was for countless other immigrants, an immigration clerk either capriciously or maliciously renamed them. The last name, Gelb, remained. Aaron became Armin and Betty became Bertha. The name Bertha has always invoked the image of a heavyset black woman belting out the blues. This was so far from my Hungarian-Jewish grandmother, who couldn't tell you who Aretha Franklin was and thought that the blues was a family of colors.

Like my paternal grandparents, my maternal grandparents wed in Europe—Hungary, to be exact. Their union was also the product of a *shidduch* (arranged marriage).

My grandfather was about eleven years older than my grandmother. She was also several inches taller than Armin. You already get the feeling that this couple was far from a perfect match.

The young Bertha was tall and thin with coal-colored wavy hair. She possessed dark, soulful eyes and a beautiful smile. Photos of my grandmother in her twenties bear a striking resemblance to my daughter, Amy. Both women carried themselves with poise and sophistication. I am told my grandmother came from an affluent family. Her father managed property for the land barons of Hungary. My grandmother received an outstanding private education and attended the best Catholic schools in her country, all the while maintaining her Jewish tradition at home.

Armin came from a respected, not particularly well-off family. His newlywed photos depict a man with slicked-back light-brown hair, a chiseled, somewhat rugged face with a strong chin and dimple, which gave rise to a slight resemblance to actor Kirk Douglas.

Armin was conscripted into the Austrian Army when still in his teens. He described his four years of military service as pure hell. Anti-Semitism among his comrades was rampant. As a Jew, he had to be diplomatic, smart, and tough; he was all three. Armin was blessed with a mechanical aptitude and good hands. As a result, he avoided direct combat by maintaining and operating the communication lines that serviced the war machines of the Austrian Empire, the same empire that would later torture, rape, and kill most of his family.

While Bertha was articulate and outgoing, Armin was quiet and shy. They escaped Europe before the Holocaust, arriving in the United States as newlyweds. They settled in New York City and had two children, my mother, Arline, and her older sister, Gloria. The sisters were close enough in age, just less than two years apart, to wrestle with a lifetime of sibling rivalry. Nonetheless, I have fond and warm memories of my Aunt Gloria and her husband, Bob.

Life in New York was tough. The Great Depression rained misery on society as a whole, and the Gelb family was no exception. Armin found it difficult to find work. This was particularly tough on my grandmother, who envisioned herself as somewhat of an aristocrat. Bertha's parents also escaped Europe before the Holocaust, and my great-grandfather, David Landesman, brought enough money to help sustain the family. A proud man, Armin found his strength was being challenged like never before. He finally secured some temporary employment in a factory where a defective machine cut off one of his fingers. His one exceptional asset, manual dexterity, was now compromised.

Armin had a cousin, Alfred Harshkovitz, who was his close boyhood friend while growing up in Hungary. Alfred also immigrated to the United States, initially settling in Chicago. The cousins eventually lost contact as they tried to build a life in a new country. Eventually Alfred relocated to Los Angeles, where he reinvented himself as Alfred Hart and began building a financial empire. Word of his success had spread, and as the Gelb family financial condition grew dismal, my grandmother urged Armin to contact his cousin to see if he had any employment opportunities for him in Los Angeles. It took some time for a response, but Hart eventually invited my grandfather to LA to talk.

Armin took a bus from New York to Los Angeles. He stayed with his Uncle Dave. Uncle Dave had come to America several years earlier and settled in Los Angeles after first giving New York a try. He warned Armin not to get involved with Hart, who was now the prosperous proprietor of Alfred Hart Distilleries, Central Liquor Distributors, and the San Angelo Wine and Spirit Corporation.

Uncle Dave told my grandfather, "Armin, Hart is a no-*gutnik*. The word is he associates with gangsters. Some say he is an associate of Meyer Lansky. If your mother were here, she would tell you that this is not the path to follow. I know that you are desperate, and you have a family to feed, but don't make a decision you will regret. Listen to me! I think I may be able to help you. Not with money, because I have very little. Here is the deal. Next month I'm moving out of Los Angeles. There is a city two or three hours east called San Bernardino. This San Bernardino is going to be a boomtown, Armin, and you and I can get in on the ground floor. Now you are probably wondering how two immigrants from Hungary with no *gelt* (money) are going to become *gonsa machors* in the next California boomtown? The blessed United States government is giving away land. All you have to do is move to San Bernardino and start a chicken farm. Are you interested?"

"Uncle Dave, if I tell Bertha to pack her bags and get the girls ready to move to San Bernardino to start a new life as chicken farmers, she will divorce me or have me locked up. Thank you, but we didn't come to America to become chicken farmers in

San Bernardino. I'll just have to take a chance on Cousin Alfred."

My grandfather had a brief meeting with Hart in his executive office. Not only had he changed his name but also his persona. He was now cold, aloof, and abrupt. The end result, however, was good. Armin now had a job. He was hired as a warehouseman or, as my grandmother called it, a crate *schlepper* (mover). Nonetheless, it was a job, and soon Bertha, my mom, and her sister, Gloria, were on a train from New York to Los Angeles for the beginning of a new life.

There were a couple of good years of employment and steady paychecks. The family lived in the West Adams section of Los Angeles. West Adams was a middle-class part of the city composed mostly of recent Jewish immigrants from Europe. Armin was still having a hard time picking up the English language. He understood English but had difficulty expressing himself, a true handicap to upward mobility.

One day the teamsters came to Al Hart Distilleries, and organizing a local union sounded good to Armin; after all, he figured Al Hart seemed to have more money than he knew what to do with. My grandfather was lifting heavy crates of liquor, engaging in the loading and unloading of freight all day. The arduous nature of the work was beginning to take its toll on Armin's back. He listened to the union organizer, who promised that with union membership came health benefits, higher salaries, and a better standard of living. As Armin listened, echoing in his mind were the countless times that Bertha would tell him, "Armin, everyone else is getting rich in California, and you are schlepping boxes and making peanuts." Soon Armin became the first union-card-carrying member of my family. A teamster nonetheless—my grandfather and Jimmy Hoffa!

When Hart got wind of Armin's union affiliation, he summoned him to his office. Armin entered the CEO's large wood paneled office, which was equipped with a wet bar that prominently displayed Hart's line of liquor. An angry looking Hart, clad in a pinstripe suit and seated in an oversized leather chair, glared through his glasses and said, "Armin, you're fired. When you came here, you were unemployed and when you walk out that door, you'll be unemployed. Let the teamsters find you a job." And, the cousins never spoke again.

Humiliated and unemployed once again, Armin wondered what he would tell Bertha. At least now she didn't have to be embarrassed to tell her friends that her husband *schlepped* boxes for a living. Thereafter, Armin had several more tough years, with intermittent occasional employment and austerity.

I heard the story of Armin's firing numerous times growing up. It was told by my parents with a sense of amusement. I loved my grandfather, and every time I heard the story I only grew angrier. As the years unfolded, my harsh feelings for Al Hart mitigated and transformed into a subtle appreciation for what he unknowingly did for my family. He in reality had a profound effect upon my life. If it weren't for Al Hart, my grandfather wouldn't have migrated to Los Angeles, and I wouldn't have been the recipient of the gift of being born and raised in Southern California.

So how did Alfred Harshkovitz become Al Hart? While Armin settled in New York, Hart somehow wound up in Chicago. Young Al Hart, according to Gus Russo in his book *Super Mob*, worked as a beer runner for the Al Capone mob. With the end of Prohibition, he landed in Los Angeles and, probably bankrolled by the mob, started several businesses relating both to the manufacturing and distribution of alcohol.

In 1952, Hart bought an interest in the beautiful Del Mar Racetrack, where, as the saying goes, the surf meets the turf. It was through his affiliation at the racetrack that Hart commenced a lifelong friendship with FBI Director J. Edgar Hoover. Hoover loved the ponies, and Hart made sure that whenever Hoover was in town he had access to the Hart Box.

In 1954, Hart took over the recently formed Beverly Hills-based City National Bank. Despite his gruff and unrefined persona, Hart was establishing himself as a legitimate businessman. By 1954, he was on the board of directors of Columbia Pictures, president and chairman of the board of City National Bank, and a major investor in gangster Bugsy Siegel's project, the Flamingo Hotel in Las Vegas. He also became a member of the exclusive Hillcrest Country Club, the city's only Jewish country club in an era when Jews were restricted from joining the city's other country clubs.

Through his bank, Hart became a major financial lender to the entertainment industry.

This enabled him to rub shoulders and develop relationships with the likes of studio executives, producers, and the leading entertainers of the time, including Frank Sinatra and countless others.

In December 1963, Sinatra turned to his friend Al Hart when his son, Frank Jr., was kidnapped and held for ransom. Hart personally went to his bank, obtained $240,000, and presented it to the FBI for a sting operation. The mission was a success, and Sinatra Jr. was freed.

A few years earlier, Sinatra had saved Hart's life. Despite not possessing the good looks of a Hollywood leading man, Hart had plenty of money, chutzpah, and a surplus of testosterone. Vic Damone was a popular recording artist in the 1950s. He was married to a beautiful young Italian-born actress named Anna Maria Pierangeli. Before marrying Damone, she was romantically involved with the actor and teenage heartthrob James Dean. Somehow Hart managed to have an affair with Pierangeli. Damone got wind of the extramarital affair and went ballistic. In Damone's biography, *Singing Was the Easy Part*, he reports that he was so enraged that he contemplated shooting Hart, whom he described in the book as a "weasily little son of a bitch," which was probably an accurate description. Sinatra intervened and protected Hart from an early burial and Damone from a murder trial and the consequences of a conviction.

The divergent lives of Al Hart and Armin Gelb continue to shape parts of my life. Every time I drive by a large office building displaying the name City National Bank, I can't help but think of how

I owe Hart for bringing my mom's family to Los Angeles and, yes, firing Armin and liberating him from being a *schlepper*. As for the now-liberated Armin, he finally got the break he had been waiting for. The postwar economy was bolstering the aircraft industry in Southern California. He was able to secure membership in the machinists' union and land a job with Douglas Aircraft in El Segundo.

Armin was great with his hands, even with a missing finger. He quickly established himself at Douglas as a valuable and skilled machinist. He was well compensated and didn't mind waking up at 4:00 a.m. to drive to work in the dark and put in long hours, including frequent overtime.

Armin took me to work with him when I was roughly six years old. It was a father-son day. He proudly wore his neatly pressed Douglas uniform: a tan shirt with matching tan pants. I thought the whole thing was a little unusual. Prior to that day, I had never seen my grandfather in a uniform. My dad, who was a trial lawyer, would go to work in Italian suits and a tie. Upon arriving at Douglas, I was surprised to see that my quiet grandfather appeared to be quite popular with his coworkers. He introduced me to his friends, who had names like Jim, John, and Peter—mostly Irish last names. After an hour or two, my grandfather joined his friends for a smoke. None of them had brought kids. My grandfather smoked Camel cigarettes. He was a chain smoker. While I loved him, I hated that smell of stale nicotine on his clothes. Armin proudly showed me the airplanes he was building.

They seemed so big, and, for a six-year-old boy who had never been in an airplane, this was an awesome experience. At the end of the day, I had a greater appreciation of who Armin was and admiration for character traits he possessed, such as an incredible work ethic, sincerity, and kindness.

As we drove out of the Douglas Aircraft parking lot, I saw my grandfather smile as he navigated his green Chevrolet from El Segundo north through the streets of Culver City. "Did you have fun today?" he asked me. "I sure did." His smile grew wider. He was a man of few words, but his broad grin spoke volumes.

Armin saved up the fruits of his labor and hours of overtime. He proudly opened a savings account at the Bank of America. He would come home every day wearing a dirty and soiled uniform. He would take it off immediately, shower, and light up several cigarettes while watching the Huntley Brinkley newscast on NBC. He would then join my grandmother in the kitchen for dinner.

My grandmother was an extraordinary cook. She would serve up stuffed cabbage with a pungent sweet-and-sour sauce, wiener schnitzel, and an extensive array of culinary delights. Upon completing dinner, Armin and Bertha would watch more television, and Armin had a few more cigarettes. He would then retire for the night. It wouldn't be long before the alarm clock would sound off, enabling him to make the 4:00 a.m. drive to Douglas Aircraft. When the alarm clock sounded, he popped out of bed like a piece of toast from a toaster, and he was ready to chase the American Dream.

Armin started real estate investing late in life and was able to purchase two apartment buildings in a desirable area of West Los Angeles. A skilled mechanic, he handled all of the plumbing and electrical work in his apartment buildings. When Armin retired from Douglas Aircraft, he and Bertha were involved in real estate management on a full-time basis.

In 1964, I traveled with my family to New York for the World's Fair. Not only did we enjoy the fair, but we got to meet my parents' remaining family and visited the places they frequented when they were young.

One of the more memorable visits was with my father's favorite uncle, Benny. Benny was my grandmother Sadie's brother. Sadie and Benny had dramatically different personalities. Benny, facially, bore a strong resemblance to my father, although he was several inches taller than my dad and about twenty-five or thirty years older. We met Benny at a small delicatessen he owned in Brooklyn, appropriately named Benny's Hebrew National. He was one of those people with a clearly visible love of life that radiated from the twinkle in his eyes and smile on his face, characteristics similar to those of my father.

It was lunchtime, and there were about five tables and a counter that sat about six. Benny's wife, a heavyset, quiet woman with a pleasant nature, was running the restaurant. Other than the Schwartz family, there was only one diner in the restaurant. Benny had his wife make us a couple of corned beef and pastrami sandwiches. He boasted that, once upon a time, you couldn't fight your way into his deli at lunchtime. The neighborhood, however, had changed. While we were scarfing down our sandwiches, Benny turned to my father and said, "Sammy, one day I'm going to be as rich as Rockefeller." I thought to myself, *He's going to have to sell a lot more corned beef and pastrami sandwiches to get into that league.*

Benny became very animated and said that the Fidel Castro regime would soon fall. Benny had invested in bonds sold by the Castro opposition. He tried to convince my dad, saying, "It will fall soon, and I will be worth millions of dollars. Sammy, I may be able to get you into the deal." My father smiled and asked Uncle Benny if he had any more pickles.

The whirlwind trip to the New York's World's Fair ended in the blink of an eye. In addition to going to the fair, we met countless relatives. As the plane left JFK Airport heading back to LAX, I was grateful that my grandparents had moved west. New York was a nice place to visit, but California bloodlines ran deep in my veins.

Upon returning to LAX, we were greeted by my grandfather Armin. He waited to assist us with our bags and drive us home. He wore his usual warm grin. His eyes always possessed a certain sadness, but that day they were sadder than usual. It clearly appeared that something important was occupying Armin's mind. After driving us home and assisting us with our luggage, he confided in my parents that while we were gone he was diagnosed with lung cancer. A several-pack-a-day smoker, he had pushed the envelope too far.

Armin had surgery a week later. A lung was removed. He seemed to be recovering and was in remission for about two years, and then my parents told me that Armin was very sick. I only saw him a couple of times after that and was told that the cancer had spread to his brain. Soon thereafter he was hospitalized, and within a short time he was dead. His was the first funeral I ever attended.

It was after his death that I learned about his sad eyes. Armin's entire immediate family was killed during the Holocaust. His mother and his youngest sister were almost able to escape while hidden by a Christian family just outside of Budapest. Just days before the emancipation, their whereabouts were discovered by a group of Nazis. My great-grandmother (Armin's mother) and my grandfather's youngest sister were brutally raped and murdered by the Nazis. The sadness of the trauma was soldered into Armin's eyes and wedged into his soul forever.

In the end, Armin left the fruits of his labor, his investment property, to Bertha, enough to keep her comfortable for the rest of her life. His life was far from a rags-to-riches story. His material riches were modest. But his life story is a good one. It is the journey of a quiet and hardworking man with sad eyes and a warm heart who, although beaten down for so many years, never gave up on himself. He finished his earthly journey attaining the dignity that he earned and deserved.

Armin, I remember you well
The sweat of a pogrom upon your face
Sailing to a new world enigmatic as
space
Armin, I remember you well
Your breath like a red tide
Smelling of smoked salmon
Armin, I remember you well
Planting the sore muscles of your soul
In the soil of the galut of
The American Dream
But America never had
A market for wise men
Leaving you sequestered,
A toolbox in one hand
And the mystery of the Zohar in the
other

And what ever happened to Uncle Benny? The Cuban Revolution never came to fruition. Benny died with an estate consisting of a surplus of unsold corned beef, pastrami, pickles, and worthless Cuban bonds. But, he had a twinkle in his eyes and a dream in the making right until the very end.

Joanne

For twenty years I walked through life as an empty vessel, seeking someone who would understand me and rain love upon my soul.

It was a hot September night. The warm desert wind, like an acoustic guitar gently finger-picking a mystical melody, kissed the swaying palm trees while the stars twinkled above. A crescent-shaped moon looked down upon me, winking, appearing to gesture that this was the genesis of something great. Indeed it was. However, not every picture is flawless. Despite the beautiful setting, it was still a fraternity party in 1970. The stage was Tucson, Arizona, the Alpha Epsilon Pi house at the University of Arizona. I was a twenty-year-old college junior. It was there that I spotted and instantly fell in love with Joanne.

She had an angelic face and beautiful, big brown eyes; her skin bore a golden tan in contrast with her honey-colored hair. I thought that she was out of my league, but what the heck? I was going to talk to her. The worst thing that could happen would be rejection, and it wouldn't be the first time.

"Hi, I'm Neil. What's your name?" She looked a little uncomfortable; I couldn't tell if she was shy or just uninterested. She responded in a soft, gentle voice, "Joanne." *Joanne*, I thought. *I like this girl, and the name seems to fit her well.* "Where are you from, Joanne?" "Chicago" she said. Okay, now the important question: *does she love baseball?* I looked into her beautiful eyes and said, "I absolutely love the Chicago Cubs. They're my favorite team next to the Dodgers." "Really?" She perked up. "That's great." Maybe she needed a little prodding. "Do you like the Cubs?" I asked. At this point, I thought I really scored: she seemed to like baseball, and we had a conversation evolving. "No," she said. "I don't like the Cubs."

The conversation came to an abrupt stop. I had to gasp as our dialogue reached a dead end. "What did you do this summer?" I ventured. "Israel," she said. "I went to Israel." "Amazing! I also went to Israel this summer." We then talked for an extended period of time, sharing our summer experiences, and so, one might say, it was Israel that brought Joanne and me together on a warm, windy, and mystical night in Tucson, Arizona, the same desert terrain that bore the voidance of my grandfather's spirit.

The next two years, 1970 and 1971, we loved and dreamed together. The counterculture and peace movements were rocking college campuses across the nation. The University of Arizona was no different, and we were center stage. Our lives were simple, like the gifts we exchanged: sweet, fragrant candles and a now-endangered species, the vinyl

WHAT IF TOMORROW NEVER COMES?

record album. While others were enthralled with the Beatles, the Stones, and the British Invasion, Joanne and I had discovered the mystical and romantic world of poet and singer Leonard Cohen. Leonard Cohen's lyrics desperately sought out the heartfelt romance that we had found in each other.

The years 1970 and 1971 sprinted right by us. We were about to graduate in the blink of an eye. Before we knew it, graduation was upon us. Joanne was hoping for a more serious and permanent relationship. As for me, I loved Joanne but wasn't prepared to commit to a lifelong relationship.

In September, I was starting law school. I was insecure about the prospect of balancing a serious romantic relationship with the demands of law school. I wasn't even certain I wanted to go to law school, but I had run out of options.

My father rendered a caveat in my senior year of college that I would have to change my lifestyle upon embarking upon my legal studies. "Neil," he said, "the law is a jealous mistress." In retrospect, I don't believe that our relationship would have survived the rigors of law school. And so Joanne returned to Chicago upon graduating from the University of Arizona, and I assumed the life of a monk in a monastery, laboriously mastering legal treatises and becoming retooled from a free-thinking dreamer to an analytical-thinking lawyer.

The time restraints of law school left little time to dream, yet one dream remained the chance of reuniting with Joanne one day and rekindling our relationship. We communicated by way of letters and phone calls, although, over time, the letters

| 39 |

and phone calls diminished in frequency. Finally, there was no communication at all. Joanne had moved and left no forwarding address. Her phone was disconnected, and her parents had an unlisted phone number.

After several months, she wrote to me, but she didn't leave a return address. She indicated that she was now in Washington, DC, teaching at a Jewish day school and enjoying it immensely. Several months passed, and I once again received a letter. This time Joanne disclosed to me that she had married a dental student. I was crushed. Her husband was attending dental school in Washington, DC, and she was continuing to teach. She said that she thought of me frequently and hoped that my life was working out. Quite frankly, my life wasn't working out. I dated a lot but couldn't find a woman who touched my soul like Joanne.

I had good dates and bad dates. Here is one of the bad ones. I was set up with a woman who had just moved from New York to Los Angeles. She had just signed a record contract with a major recording label. My friend said that she was going to be the next Barbara Streisand and was absolutely gorgeous. "Treat her right," he said. "A catch like this doesn't come around more than once in a life time." I proceeded to contact a ticket broker to get concert tickets at the Hollywood Bowl and requested the best box seats available. I don't recall who the artist was that was performing, but I paid an outrageous premium, and we received an excellent box.

I nervously arrived at her West Hollywood apartment to pick her up for the big night. My friend was right: she was gorgeous. As we drove to the Hollywood Bowl, she engaged in a monologue. Her New York accent was thick, and her delivery unrefined. She spoke nonstop with no interest in a dialogue. I don't recall too much more about the evening except for the following: The concert had just started. We were sharing the box with a couple we didn't know. It appeared as if they were on a date. The man was about ten years older than me. I was probably twenty-five at the time. He was broad-shouldered and several inches taller than me. I was five feet, nine inches tall, and he must have been six-foot-one or six-foot-two. He had an attractive date. There was no interaction between us prior to the concert. The other couple continued talking once the concert started. My date proceeded to ask the couple to shut up. Certainly if this situation had been approached a little more diplomatically, it would not have escalated.

The big, burly guy looked at my date with contempt. He continued talking to the young woman he was with and seemed to raise his voice louder. My date then responded with the following words: "Shut the fuck up." I was growing increasingly uncomfortable with the situation. The burly guy retorted, "What did you say?" My date repeated the words, "Shut the fuck up." At that point I felt as if the entire Hollywood Bowl was now focused upon our box.

My date turned to me and said, "Do something. You're not going to let him speak to me like this, are you? What are you gonna do?" The only thing I really wanted to do was become invisible. I paused for a moment then looked at the burly guy and my date and said, "Let's forget this ever happened. Start over and enjoy the concert." While there was tension for the remainder of the show, there were no more verbal exchanges. As for my date and me, the remainder of the evening was draped in silence. The verbal drought ended when I walked her to the front door of her apartment, and matter-of-factly she mumbled, "Goodnight," and our relationship never went beyond that evening.

This dating experience was so unlike my time with Joanne. With her, everything came so naturally and flowed with the tranquility of her glowing soul. I had now graduated law school and began practicing law. But I felt I had an empty life and regretted losing something precious. Then, out of nowhere, I received a late-night phone call. It was Joanne, and she was whispering. She said that she and her husband had moved to Pittsburgh, and her husband was now practicing dentistry. She told me how much she loved me and missed me. I responded, "But you are married." She replied that her marriage was a nightmare and that she was trying to get out of the relationship and then abruptly hung up. Now how was I supposed to go back to sleep? No address, no phone number, a husband—this wasn't a good situation.

Every couple of weeks, the scenario repeated itself. More details were disclosed about the horrible relationship from which she couldn't escape. She would express her love to me and then abruptly hang up. The phone calls eventually stopped, and Joanne disappeared again.

Then, several months later, I received another phone call. This time it was different. It was a Sunday morning. She wasn't whispering. Joanne informed that she was now divorced and living at home with her parents in Chicago. She was planning a trip to Los Angeles to visit a friend. I offered to pick her up at the airport. She gave me the date and flight information. When she got off the plane, I immediately spotted her, and she was more beautiful than ever. I brought her to my apartment in Westwood, and we never parted. As for the friend in LA she was coming to see, she informed me that I was the only friend she had in Los Angeles.

Every morning she would play the soundtrack from *Annie*: "The sun will come out tomorrow, bet your bottom dollar that tomorrow there will be sun." I watched her from a distance drinking coffee, her eyes teary as she listened to the song. An unhappy marriage, disappointed parents, and an undefined future. As I stared at her, I knew I loved her. If she could love me as much as I loved her then the sun would indeed rise for both of us. Within a few days we knew that we would never be apart again. Joanne found a job teaching at The Temple Emanuel Jewish Day School in Beverly Hills. We were both once again happy and in love.

Several months before we reunited, my grandmother Bertha, who had just recently passed away prior to Joanne's coming to Los Angeles, asked me, "Whatever became of your girlfriend in Arizona?" As my communication with Joanne had been cut off at the time, I responded to Bertha that sometimes in life we make mistakes; mine was allowing Joanne to get away. On August 25, 1979, a year after Joanne arrived in Los Angeles, we married. I was the luckiest and happiest guy in the world. Not only was she a beautiful woman, but, more importantly, she had a radiant soul that shined with love and kindness.

A large contingency of her family from Chicago came out to Los Angeles for the wedding. We had a small ceremony, including family and a few friends. The wedding was held at Stephen Wise Temple in Bel Air, a beautiful temple nestled in the Santa Monica Mountains. During the ceremony, I noticed an elderly woman who bore a slight resemblance to Bertha standing off to the side. She held herself up with a cane. She wasn't part of the Chicago contingency, and she certainly wasn't anyone I knew. She disappeared immediately after the ceremony. Later, my sister, Leslie, approached me and asked who the elderly woman standing off to the side was. Leslie said, "She looked so much like Bertha." The mystery woman's identity was never discovered.

Joanne became pregnant with Scott several months after our wedding. She finished the school year in June and then took an extended hiatus from teaching and became a full-time mom. We purchased our first home in September 1980 in Northridge, California.

A broad-shouldered, blond-haired, brown-eyed, nine-pound Scott Alan Schwartz entered the world on December 14, 1980. He looked just like his mother. Joanne didn't want to let go of him. She couldn't believe that she was a mother for the first time at thirty-one years old. She loved motherhood. Nine months later, Joanne was pregnant again. She was ecstatic with the prospect of having a second child. But on Christmas Eve day, she called me at my office, crying. "Neil, I'm spotting heavily. No, actually I'm bleeding heavily; I think I'm having a miscarriage." She was ending her first trimester and in her third month of pregnancy.

I drove home and picked Joanne up. We dropped Scott off at my parents' home and proceeded to her OB/GYN in Century City. I was driving like I was at the Indianapolis 500, breaking every speed limit in the City of Los Angeles. We arrived at his office at three-fifty in the afternoon of Christmas Eve. The doctor performed an outpatient dilation and curettage. Joanne came out of the procedure with a smile on her face, holding back her disappoint-ment. "Well, Neil," she said, "I guess it just wasn't meant to be. Let's go out to dinner." There was a Hamburger Hamlet next door to the doctor's office. We had dinner, and she talked about how lucky she was that we had Scott. She said if she never had another child, she was content because she felt that she was blessed. She then added that a few more would make her even happier.

Three years after Scott's birth, we were blessed with the birth of Amy. She looked quite different from her brother. She had jet-black hair, dark skin, brown eyes, and favored me rather than Joanne. And so our family was complete: a boy, a girl, and some wonderful years ahead. They went by far too quickly.

Tough Road for the Judge

A year after Amy's birth, my father, who was now a superior court judge in Los Angeles, experienced a life-threatening heart attack. He was at home with my mother in the evening when he experienced extreme difficulty breathing and chest pain. My mom called 911, and my father was rushed to Sherman Oaks Hospital. It was nip and tuck, but he made it. My father had always been the pillar of strength for our family. He was my mentor and confidante. He was now in a crisis situation. The heart attack had left him too weakened to have the quadruple bypass surgery that he required. He had significant heart damage. As a prerequisite to surgery, he had to recover from the heart attack and enter a cardiac rehabilitation program.

I remember I was present when my dad met with the heart surgeon. The doctor's office was located in the Cedars Sinai Medical Tower in Los Angeles. The doctor was a big, husky guy who looked more like a retired NFL lineman than one of Los Angeles's leading heart surgeons. My father said, "Doc, when you say this surgery involves risk, what do you mean? Every surgery has risk." "Well, Judge," he said, "your heart is damaged, and you have four arteries totally occluded. It's a miracle you're still alive. If we don't operate, I don't give you more than two months to live. If we operate, because of your weakened heart and the complexity of the surgery, there is a risk, and a significant one, that you'll die on the operating table. If you make it through the surgery, you'll have a new lease on life." My father looked at the doctor, gave him a warm smile, and responded, "Well, Doctor, I have no choice then. I love life, and I love my family. Let's proceed with the surgery."

I recall sitting with my mother; my brother, Randy; and my sister, Leslie, for about twelve hours during the surgical procedure and post-op ICU. Joanne was at home with the kids. Scott was about four years old and Amy about a year old.

During a lengthy surgery, when thoughts of death and loss stare you in the eye, uncertainty paints the next moment. It is within this setting that one can more readily change gears and peel off the layers of time. I reflected upon my father's life and the way he lived it to the fullest. He always had different projects and entrepreneurial pursuits outside of his law practice. But, most of all, he was always there for me to assist in the navigation process of crossing life's narrow and unsteady bridge.

In 1960, Dad started a record company. It was an exciting era, early rock 'n' roll. My dad took me to several recording sessions. I was only ten at the time. But after watching my first recording session, I knew that I now had a dream. Yes, the dream that much of America would soon share: to become a rock star. My dad bought me a guitar. I took lessons, listened to lots of radio, and bought stacks of records, dreaming that one day people would be listening to me.

My father's partner in the record label, Norty Beckman, was a heavyset, messy-looking, but always cheerful fellow. Norty owned the legendary Norty's Record Store on Fairfax Avenue in Los Angeles located across the street from Canter's Deli. The record company generated volumes of fun and lots of debt.

Dad met Norty through Democratic politics, where they were both active in the Adlai Stevenson presidential campaign pitting the liberal Democrat against the Republican candidate, war hero Dwight D. Eisenhower, and his conservative running mate, Richard Nixon. Later, both Norty and my father were active on the Los Angeles County Presidential Committee for John Kennedy for President.

Soon thereafter, politics took center stage as my dad became active in the Kennedy for President Campaign. The Democratic National Convention was held in Los Angeles in the summer of 1960. My father took me and my brother, Randy, to hear John F. Kennedy give his nomination acceptance speech. I was hypnotized by the power of this great orator and moved by the things he had to say.

As I continued to wait in the hospital, there were still no reports other than dad was in post-surgical ICU and not ready for visitors. My mind continued to drift back in time as we anxiously waited to learn his fate.

Life Lessons from My Dad, Bar Mitzvah, and Little League Baseball

In the department store of life, baseball is in the toy department. I have had a lifelong romance with the sport. The relationship, however, began on an unsteady foundation. The tenuous beginning was as follows. At nine years old, I nervously accompanied my father to Rancho Park, located on the west side of Los Angeles. The event was little league tryouts. I stood in amazement, staring at a sea of kids. It seemed like there were a million.

The competition was keen and my skill level poor. I left the tryouts discouraged and humiliated. "Dad, how did these kids get so good?" "Hard work, Neil, hard work. Life requires hard work in order to succeed. Success will not come to you. You have to work to attain it." And so on a disappointing day in April of 1959, I was introduced to the American work ethic—an introduction that was made possible by America's favorite pastime, baseball.

Two weeks after tryouts, several friends at school announced that they had been drafted. "The

Red Sox," one proudly declared; "The Yankees," boasted another. Saddened but not surprised, I knew I hadn't made the cut. That night at dinner, looking into my father's eyes, I knew that he felt my pain. "Don't give up," he said. "Don't give up. I'm sure there are still open roster spots to fill." The spots were all filled, but my father was about to create one.

A few nights later at dinner, Dad said, "Neil, congratulations. You were drafted by the Braves." I couldn't believe it. It must have been a mistake or an error in judgment by someone who clearly should have known better. The person who should have known better turned out to be my dad's client. He was a party to a contentious and costly divorce. He was also the manager of the Cheviot Hills Braves. At nine years old, I was introduced to the concept of *quid pro quo.*

I practiced hard, but when you have poor reflexes and lack of coordination the best solution is probably a different hobby. But my father's words, "Work hard; don't give up," rang loud in my head. Unfortunately, hard work and a positive attitude couldn't overcome my lack of ability.

I entered most games in the last inning because the league had a rule mandating that every player had to play. Right field was reserved for the worst of the worst. That was me! The manager summoned me into action the last inning of every game. As I ran out to take my place in right field, my lips became cold and turned purple, my stomach churned, and my heart fluttered.

Right field was my first religious experience. I prayed fervently to The Almighty: "Please don't let anybody hit a ball anywhere near me." And my prayers were answered through the assistance of a chubby, cherub-faced, blond-haired kid with a crew-cut—our team's pitcher. He had a difficult time getting the ball over the plate, and a parade of walks ensued. I was safe.

I never spoke with my teammate pitcher; however, his face shared the same painful expression I wore upon entering the game. As you might have imagined, I didn't win the most valuable player award. Nor did our pitcher win the Cy Young Award. He did, however, win another award: the Academy Award for best actor. His name? Jeff Bridges.

I would be remiss in not acknowledging the player I relieved in right field. His name was Bobby Rodriguez, and he never won an Academy Award. However, in 2008, *Money* magazine named him the best mutual fund manager of our time. He successfully managed $16 billion dollars for the FPA Capital Fund Family. I don't recall talking to Bobby much. Perhaps I might have asked him the score of the game because even then he seemed smart. I guess I should have asked him for some stock tips, but who knew?

I played several more years of little league. I worked hard and honed my skills. The quality of my game improved each year. At age twelve, I was a proud member of the all-star team. I loved playing baseball so much that I would spend long summer days riding my bicycle to Rancho Park to meet other kids who shared the same passion for the game. While the smell of freshly cut grass and the imperfectly manicured infield was not Dodger Stadium, it was my fantasy big league playing field.

Rancho Park was located on Motor Avenue. When I was done playing ball for the day, I would frequently ride my bike north on Motor Avenue, where 20th Century Fox Studios stood tall at the intersection of Pico Boulevard and Motor Avenue. On the southeast corner of Pico Boulevard and Motor Avenue was the Hillcrest Country Club, playground to the rich and famous.

Riding my bike south on Motor Avenue, I would navigate to Washington Boulevard, home of MGM and now Sony Pictures. As I pedaled, I thought about the future. What would I be? What was in store for my life? And I also pondered, *What if tomorrow never comes?* I didn't really want to focus on that concept too long, so my mind wandered to images of some of the cute girls in my class. And I just kept pedaling.

Our home in Cheviot Hills was near the Pico Robertson area. I would sometimes accompany my mother on Friday afternoons for some shopping. To some, the Pico Robertson area is a Borscht Belt. For others, it's the hood. For me, it was in some ways my home away from home. My grandparents Armin and Bertha Gelb resided in the Borscht Belt, as did my Aunt Gloria and Uncle Bob and their two daughters, my cousins Candy and Ilene. Also in the Borscht Belt was Congregation Mogen David, where I attended Hebrew school.

The first stop on the Friday afternoon shopping junket with my mother was at Beverlywood Bakery. We took a number at the counter and seemed to wait an eternity. The wait, however, was tolerable, as I would joyfully inhale the sweet scent of freshly baked goods. It wouldn't take long before a friendly woman behind the counter would spot me and offer me samplings of incredibly delicious and warm cookies. Biting into a cookie, I thought, *Neil, life is good.* We usually left with a challah and a couple of pink boxes packed with Danishes, black-and-white cookies, and cake. Who was counting calories or carbs back then? Not my family.

The next stop was Charlie's Deli. It was a little hole in the wall. But Charlie made the best chopped liver in the city. And my dad loved chopped liver. The poor guy didn't have a chance after clogging his arteries with a lifetime consumption of chopped liver and his mother's fatty chicken soup.

We then began the drive home, west to Cheviot Hills. Our destination: Cavendish Drive. For most people the drive would have been five or ten minutes. But Mom never liked to go faster than twenty-five miles an hour. We spent a lot of time in the car as kids.

Cheviot Hills was a vibrant and upwardly mobile community with young families and lots of kids. Most garages had a station wagon. Much to my sister's dismay, we never got one. The neighborhood had a real "Leave It to Beaver" vibe about it. In fact, Barbara Billingsly, who played June Cleaver, Wally and the Beaver's mother on the show, lived around the corner from us.

Residing on the corner of Cavendish and Cheviot Drive were Michael and Jeff Maurer. They were the grandsons of Moe Howard of "The Three Stooges." Moe appeared to be a good grandfather and would visit frequently. On occasion, he picked Mike and Jeff up from our elementary school, Castle Heights. The Stooges may have been at the peak of their popularity at that time, and Moe's appearance at school caused a near riot. Moe usually wore a sporty hat, obscuring his trademark bangs.

My sister, Leslie, had a friend named Zana, who lived about a block away from the Maurers' home. Zana's father was a science-fiction writer. He didn't drive a car. He was one of the early environmentalists. His name didn't mean much to me then: Ray Bradbury. Ray would rely upon his wife, public transportation, or his bicycle to get him around the city. And it is probable that, for a brief moment, Ray Bradbury might have peddled by Moe Howard at the corner of Cavendish and Cheviot, where science fiction and slapstick comedy intersected in a blink of the eye, which surely must have caused a cosmic explosion. This leads me to my days in religious school.

Hebrew School Days

Congregation Mogen David, home to my Hebrew school, was housed in a brick building on Pico Boulevard, adjacent to Beverly Hills to the north, Century City to the west, and Pico Robertson to the east. Class was held on Tuesdays and Thursdays from 4:00 p.m. to 6:00 p.m. and on Sunday mornings from 10:00 a.m. to 12:00 p.m. I'm not sure which was worse, the evening weekday classes after suffering through a day in secular school or Sunday mornings, which righteously interfered with one of my great joys: sleeping in. They called Hebrew school Talmud-Torah. I don't know why. We never studied Talmud and were minimally exposed to Torah.

We were usually late to Hebrew school. With my mother at the wheel, it was a long and slow drive. If she would only have turned the radio dial to play some good old rock and roll. No, Mom had her favorite beautiful music station, KPOL. We were always the last ones to arrive to class. I think I broke the record for Hebrew school tardiness.

I was in a carpool with my classmate and friend Neal Weinberg. He spells his name with an "a," and I spell mine with an "i." He told me that his parents spelled his name that way so he wouldn't get confused with the "i" before "e" rule. I didn't quite understand the logic to that, but I also never understood the "i" before "e" rule.

Having two boys with identical-sounding names in the class was confusing to our teachers. So one year the teacher addressed me as "Neil Brown Eyes" and Neal Weinberg as "Neal Blue Eyes." Needless to say, it didn't take long before my classmates were addressing me as "Neil Brown Eyes." This didn't carry over well onto the playground at recess time.

Neal's mom, Sylvia, or dad, Abe, would pick us up from Hebrew school. Sylvia had a station wagon, which was always fun to ride in, and both his parents drove well over twenty-five miles an hour. I don't know who disliked Hebrew school more: me or Neal Weinberg. I guess I actually did; Neal became a rabbi.

It was apparent that our Hebrew school teachers wanted to be there less than we did. They were mostly middle-aged Israeli women who had a poor command of the English language and even less control of their classroom.

At times I actually felt sorry for these women as they attempted to teach us about the Philistines and Canaanites. I couldn't figure out who these guys were and what relevance they had to my life. Meanwhile, hell was breaking loose in the back of the classroom, where major spitball exchanges were being tendered. Not everyone was a spitball warrior. There were two or three guys who would find an obscure corner and listen to rock and roll music on transistor radios equipped with earpieces. The more diligent students brought their homework from secular school. And there was one student who was a prolific reader. Each class session he would bring a *Playboy* magazine, which he would keep well hidden on his lap and under the desk. Periodically he would look up and flash an innocent smile at the teacher.

The highlight of class was the 5:00 p.m. recess. The teachers would lock the doors to their classrooms, leaving the students tightly secured and restricted to the confines of the room. The teachers would then congregate in the hall, smoke cigarettes, and discuss in Hebrew their disdain for their students.

Fast forward to three years later: At twelve years old, I anxiously awaited my bar mitzvah. The culmination of four years of Hebrew school was drawing near. Soon the Philistines and Canaanites would be out of my life. Soon I would be able to sleep in again on Sundays.

My parents arranged for a bar mitzvah tutor to come to the house. I remember him well. He was an elderly gentleman who wore a black fedora that partially deflected focus from his acne-scarred face. He wore a baggy black suit. The collar of his jacket was lighty dusted by dandruff flakes. His breath was bad, and he spoke in a rapid-fire style with a New York accent. "I'm going to chant your Haftorah (Torah portion of the week). Listen carefully!" He chanted in a nasal, dissonant tone. Amazingly, no glass broke, and our house was intact. "In a few

months you will chant your Haftorah just like me."
I had dreams of being the lead singer in a rock and
roll band, but now I had a voice coach bent on
teaching me to sing like a sick coyote.

"I've made you a tape," he said. "Study the tape,
practice, and work on trying to sound like me.
G-d willing, you'll do terrific. See you next week."
And so I worked hard, made progress, and started
sounding like him.

About six weeks before my bar mitzvah, the
rabbi called my father. "Sammy," he said, "I have to
see you and Neil immediately." My father replied,
"Is something wrong?" "A small problem," said the
rabbi, "nothing serious. Can you meet me Sunday
morning at ten in my study?" I was very nervous,
fearful that the tutor felt I wasn't progressing fast
enough and needed another year of training.

On Sunday morning, my dad and I met the
rabbi in his study. His name was Abe Maron. He
was a short man with a boxy build and a sincere
warmth and kindness about him. The rabbi wore
thick glasses, and when he looked at you he always
appeared to be squinting. "Neil," he said, "I'd like
to hear you chant your Haftorah." Just as I sus-
pected: the big test. With fear and in trepidation, I
proceeded. The rabbi immediately interrupted me,
sharply saying, "Just as I thought. We have a problem. We had to terminate the bar mitzvah tutor.
It turned out he taught several of his students the
wrong Haftorah portion. The Haftorah that Neil
has learned is not for the week of his bar mitzvah."
My always-optimistic and resourceful father asked,
"What can we do about this, Rabbi? Can we change

his bar mitzvah date?" "Unfortunately, no, Sammy. The problem is that the Haftorah Neil learned was read last week." I listened and thought, *This is bad news. With only six weeks to go, I have to start all over again.*

"Neil, I'm going to have our new cantor, Leopold Snzeer, contact you immediately. It's summer vacation. You aren't planning on a vacation or summer camp, are you?" "No," I said. Silently I thought that this was really going to cut down on my baseball time. "You will study with the cantor daily, learn the new Haftorah, and do a great job. I have confidence in you and can tell you're a smart kid. Your voice isn't so great, but you don't want to be a cantor when you grow up, do you?" "No." I smiled. "That's good," said the rabbi with a big grin. "What do you want to be?" "I have dreams of pitching for the Dodgers, maybe becoming the next Sandy Koufax."

The rabbi's squinting became more pronounced, and a wide smile emerged on his face. He turned his head and glanced at my father. He then turned his head and focused his squinty eyes upon me. "I once had a dream. I wanted to play shortstop for the New York Yankees," he said. "Instead I went to the Yeshiva. But I still dreamed. Neil, dreams are important. They renew the spirit and give us purpose and meaning in our lives. Never stop dreaming. And if you do pitch for the Dodgers, don't forget the old rabbi. Box seats behind home plate would be just fine."

Meeting the Cantor

My mother drove at her usual slow speed to my first tutorial with the cantor. I asked her to remind me of his last name. It was an unusual name that I was having problems with. "Snzeer," she said. "What?" I asked. She lowered the car radio. Again, she said, "Snzeer. It rhymes with *shmeer*. You know, Neil, you *shmeer* cream cheese on a bagel. Come to think about it, forget what I told you; you might accidentally call him Shmeer. Just call him Cantor."

We arrived at temple late for my first class with the cantor. My mother escorted me. I was very nervous. Upon entering the classroom, we were warmly greeted by a distinguished-looking man with brown hair with a little gray starting to show. He was dressed impeccably in a well-tailored suit and beautiful silk tie. He looked more like a CEO of a Fortune 500 company than a Cantor Snzeer. He flashed a warm smile and extended his arm to greet me with a strong handshake. His eyes shined brightly. He spoke with a strong European accent and interjected a lot of Yiddish, most of which I didn't understand.

It was apparent that he wanted to be in this time and place at this moment. "So, Neil, it's so nice to meet you and get you ready for your bar mitzvah." "Thank you, Rabbi. It's nice to meet you." "Thanks for the promotion, but I'm the cantor, not the rabbi." "That's okay because 'rabbi' means 'teacher,' so you're close." At least I didn't call him Cantor Schmeer.

"I hear that your voice is changing," he said. "Most of my bar mitzvah boys have this issue. I remember that, as a child, I sang like an angel. I loved to sing, and at an early age I knew that I wanted to be a cantor. But right before my bar mitzvah, my voice started to change. I lost the ability to sing beautifully. But it was just a phase of life. In life we go through many phases. Life can be like a rollercoaster ride. Oy vey, now I'm starting to sound like a rabbi." Suddenly, the cantor closed his eyes and began to hum a melody in his post-pubescent voice. I quietly waited for our session to resume.

The cantor slowly ended his chant, opened his eyes, and looked towards me, saying, "Let me tell you one more thing before we start to practice your Haftorah. As a bar mitzvah boy, you chant the Haftorah, and I know that you will do so beautifully. You will also give a speech. There is a difference between words and music. Used properly, they both elevate people to a higher level of being. In Yiddish, we say *shana verta* (beautiful words). Oy! With *shana verta*, you can inspire people, provoke them to deep and meaningful thinking. Neil, your bar mitzvah speech will shine with *shana verta*. Your father and the rabbi will work with you on your speech. They will show you how to paint pictures with words. I will teach you the *tropes* (melodies to chant the Haftorah). And where words end, music begins. With the right melodic vibration, a soul can be touched. In six weeks you will paint the picture with your words and find and deliver the melody of your soul."

Six weeks later, the cantor shepherded me to the *bima* (a raised platform in a synagogue). I hit a home run with my explanation of the Haftorah portion and even wove in some *shana verta*.

I made it through the chanting of my Haftorah, avoiding breaking the stained-glass windows of the *shul*. My nasal voice frequently cracked. Upon the conclusion of the service, several congregants approached me at the Kiddush lunch that followed the service. They wished me *mazel tov*, adding, "Your speech was great but your singing voice? Ah, you don't want to be a cantor anyway, do you?"

I was blessed to have Cantor Szneer as a teacher. I was equally fortunate for many years to come to listen to his soulful *davening* (praying) at Congregation Mogen David. His voice resonated with such emotion that you could feel heaven shaking, angels dancing, and earthly voyagers marveling. To hear him *daven* was a "wow" moment, a spiritually moving experience.

The cantor attended my wedding and Scott's *bris* (circumcision). Over the years I regrettably lost touch with him. However, I will always remember Cantor Szneer as one of my most influential teachers and a world-class cantor.

I appreciated Cantor Szneer even more when I learned later in life about the journey he took and his escape from *galut*. The cantor was born in Munich, Germany. His early childhood was good. He had a dream of one day becoming both a cantor and a teacher. That dream was interrupted on November 9, 1938, one of the darkest days in modern Jewish history. It became known as Kristallnacht. Leopold was sixteen years old at the time. His life changed overnight as he watched Nazis burn synagogues and Jewish-owned stores.

Thousands of Jews were rounded up and taken to Dachu and other concentration camps in Germany. Young Leopold was arrested and sent to a concentration camp; he escaped and spent some time with the resistance and later on his own. He hid in forests and abandoned structures, fearing every moment that the dark forces of evil were just around the corner.

Time passed, and the "liberation" arrived. The joy of freedom was soon dampened with the realization that his parents, most of his family, and many of his closest friends were now dead. Yes, he was free, but he stood in torn clothing, without possessions and with little family. He was now faced with rebuilding his broken world. And that he did, with a smile on his face and a song in his heart. His legacy will be that of both a survivor and a master teacher in the highest sense of the word.

I remember how, as I sat in *shul* (synagogue) with my father, Dad would close his eyes, with his face displaying contentment while listening to this great cantor. He would then open his eyes and whisper, "Remember this melody and store it in your heart and in your mind for the darkest of times for inspiration." And that I did.

⋅━◉⧽⋅

As my family and I sat in the hospital, waiting for news about my father, countless memories ran through my head, all good. I thought to myself, *I can't lose this guy; he has been my Rock of Gibraltar. He's tough, he will persevere, and he will emerge from the canvas before the ten count.* I hoped and prayed that he would come out of the surgery alive and make a complete recovery. And he did. He proceeded to live another seven years, not the best-quality years, but he lived and enjoyed each day.

About two years after the open-heart surgery, he experienced renal failure, which required kidney dialysis. Despite this burdensome necessity, he managed to continue working as a judge in between bouts of congestive heart failure that required short hospital stays. The twinkle in his eyes that signified his passion for life began to diminish. Nonetheless, he never complained, although his verbose nature began to manifest brevity. A friend of mine who was a student of the Kabala once told me that each human being is programmed to speak a certain number of words in his lifetime. I assumed that my wise father knew this and, with his growing silence, was engaged in budgeting and trying to extend his life.

Finally, in 1991, my father retired from the bench and once again was scheduled for a high-risk heart surgery. This time it was to replace a valve. Again, the family congregated for many hours in the coronary surgical waiting room. And this time I wasn't so sure that the old champ would be able to rise from the canvas before the count of ten.

The husky surgeon who skillfully performed the quadruple-bypass surgery seven years before was now retired. The new heart surgeon was a tall, tanned physician with movie-star good looks. At the conclusion of the surgery, he told us that Dad was alive and seemed to be doing well. He then cautioned us that because of his poor overall condition he was at high risk for complications. They would watch him carefully in ICU recovery.

Soon thereafter, my father progressed to regular ICU. He spoke a little when we saw him there. The surgeon told us that Dad was doing great but had a slight fever. He assured us that it was normal. He anticipated a full recovery and a better quality of life. We were ecstatic. In the meantime, the doctor said he was going to Aspen, Colorado, for a skiing trip for about two weeks. His associate would watch over Dad.

As the surgeon ascended the ski slopes of Aspen, my father's temperature also ascended and climbed dangerously. An infectious-disease doctor was summoned. They administered several antibiotics intravenously. No one or any antibiotic could stop the raging fever. It was apparent that my father was fading. He slept most of the time and occasionally opened his eyes. I attempted to give him the same words of encouragement he had so frequently given to me in life. "Dad, you're going to make it. You have to make it." His eyes teared up, and he looked into my eyes, just staring. I wish I knew what he was thinking. His last thoughts. I was waiting for his last words of wisdom. But no words were spoken. My father, my mentor, my source of strength closed his eyes and took the quintessential journey the next day.

The Search for Murray

As we prepared to make arrangements for the funeral, I spoke with my brother about our contacting Uncle Murray to tell him that his brother had passed away. I was delegated the task of calling Murray. It had been many years since my father and Murray had spoken. After I dialed his number, a young woman answered his phone. I asked to speak with Murray Schwartz. "He doesn't live here anymore. Who is this?" she asked. "It's his nephew Neil Schwartz," I said. "I'm calling to inform him that his brother, Sam, has died." The young woman said, "He lives in a retirement home, but I don't know where. Actually, he's in the hospital now." "Hospital?" I said. "Which hospital?" She said she didn't know. I then asked her who she was. "I'm Byron's girlfriend," she said. Byron was Murray's adopted son. I asked her to give Byron the funeral information. "Okay," she responded, and the conversation ended.

I never saw Byron at the funeral. If I did, I wouldn't have recognized him, having seen him only perhaps twice when we were both children. Nevertheless, I was deeply touched upon reading the guest book at the funeral and noting the signature of Byron Schwartz.

After completion of sitting *shivah* for my father, I felt compelled to see Murray, which was no easy task. *Shivah* in Jewish tradition is a weeklong mourning period following burial of the deceased. It is observed for first-degree relatives: fathers, mothers, sons, daughters, brothers, sisters, and spouses. Other family members and friends visit the home of the mourners, lending emotional support and comfort to those grieving.

The quest to find Murray began. I called his home a couple of times, but the phone just rang endlessly; there was no answering machine. I decided to check hospitals. I first called Cedar Sinai Hospital, where my father had been. I was lucky and attained success on the first call. I contacted my brother, Randy, brought him up to speed, and we were immediately off to Cedar Sinai Hospital to see Uncle Murray, not knowing what condition we would find him in or how he would respond to seeing his estranged nephews. He probably hadn't seen us in over twenty years. Yet this was the way my father would have wanted us to handle the situation. In addition, I, too, needed some closure in the schism between Murray and my father. It was too late for my dad, but Randy and I were on a mission of reconciliation; we were my father's emissaries.

We found our way to the hospital room where Murray was staying. I found him much the same way I remembered him but older and still smiling. "Uncle Murray," I said, "Neil and Randy Schwartz, your nephews. We are here to see you. May we visit with you a little bit?" "Sure, boys," he said, smiling all the while. "I can't believe what handsome young men you've become; you sure don't get it from your dad. Where does the time go?" "How are you, Uncle Murray?" "Oh, my diabetes has been flaring up on me and giving me some problems, but I'm better and hope to get out of here in a day or two." "Unfortunately, we have some bad news for you. Our dad has died." "What?" he cried out. "Sammy is dead?" He burst into tears. I saw, in the opening of the floodgate of endless tears, regrets for what could have been in their relationship. "We're sorry," we said. Just then a nurse walked in to draw blood. "Gentlemen, you will have to step outside now." As Murray regained his composure, he said, "Thanks for coming, boys. I appreciate it, and I'm sorry for your loss." "Thanks," we said.

We left, and I never saw Uncle Murray again. However, we discovered with great irony that at the time of Dad's death, both brothers, Murray and Sam, were both hospitalized at Cedar Sinai Hospital, on the same floor and just a few rooms from each other.

A few months later, while casually skimming the obituary section of the *Los Angeles Times*, I saw the name Murray Schwartz, husband of the late Sophie Schwartz and father of Bryon Schwartz. Upon reading the obituary, I once again contacted my brother and sister and asked them if they wanted to attend the funeral with me. Several hours later, the three of us attended Murray's funeral. It was small, with about twenty-five people. I hoped to gain greater insight into the elusive life of my uncle, but the rabbi who officiated didn't even have the right name for him. He repeatedly referred to Morry Schwartz. A brief biography of Murray was read, but there was no picture showing the essence of who he was.

As with Cain and Abel, there was never peace between Sam and Murray. My father sought peace, but Murray, for whatever reason, wasn't interested in the reconciliation. Whether Murray ever found peace in his life, I will never know. How often he thought of his daughter, whom he gave up for adoption, I will never know. When I think of my dad's family, it provokes numerous questions. Would Ziggy's life have been different if he married a different woman? Would things have been different if he came to grips with his alcoholism and sought intervention?

Would my grandmother Sadie's life have been different if she married another man rather than Ziggy? Or, regardless of her partner, would the firm grip of depression forever have colored her life? Would the modern advent of anti-depressive medication have made a difference? Would she have averted a lifetime battling depression if she remained in New York, connected to her brothers and sisters and the Orthodox community?

As for my father, he somehow escaped the *galut* that imprisoned his parents. He found peace within himself and in his family. He found purpose in life.

My mother lived until October 2008. She was eighty-two years old when she checked out, outliving my father by seventeen years. A bright woman, she played bridge twice a week until she was eighty years old. She was a vociferous reader, articulate, and charming. This personality profile made it difficult to accept how Alzheimer's disease tore down her brain in just a matter of time. In the end, she rarely knew who she was or where she was.

And so, in October 2008, I began to look at the world differently. My parents were now both deceased, I was the eldest of three children, as well as a husband and the father of two young adults. Life was moving too quickly.

The Next Generation Grows Up

Scott was now a practicing attorney, and Amy was working as a production assistant on the CBS television comedy series "How I Met Your Mother." She had graduated from The University of California at Santa Barbara with a degree in film. While still a student, she obtained a summer internship on comedian Tom Green's short-lived talk show. A writer on the show spotted the attractive young intern with jet-black hair, big brown eyes, and an electrifying smile. He crafted a way to get her in front of the camera. He approached her and congratulated her on becoming the "gum girl." Tom Green disliked gum chewers in his audience. Amy's new role was to walk up and down the audience aisle with a large jar in which audience members could dispose of their gum. She carried out the task at the beginning of each show, all the while maintaining her signature smile. And, of course, Tom even said, "Hey, let's give a big hand for Amy the Gum Girl." The summer ended, and it was time to go back to school and learn more about film theory, not an easy transition after being in front of the camera, no less as the gum girl.

Amy had one more in-front-of-the-camera experience. Her uncle, television and film director Dan Sackheim, was directing a movie, *The Glass House*. Amy was a high school student at the time. Dan had a perfect role for her, playing a high school student with only one or two lines. The speaking part for her first and last film wound up on the editor's floor. But there are two scenes in the movie where you see Amy walking on campus. I'm embarrassed to say how many times Joanne and I watched that movie just to see her.

Amy in Love
(2007)

It became apparent that there were no foreseeable promotions in sight at "How I Met Your Mother," so Amy jumped ship and began working as a production and casting assistant on several reality TV shows and eventually on a pilot for a sitcom. It was there that she met Joe Port or Joey, as she called him. Joey was the executive producer of the show, and Amy was his assistant. They didn't date during the production. But I could tell for the first time in Amy's life that she was in love. She would constantly drop Joey's name with references like, "He's such a nice guy" or that he was the nicest boss she ever worked for. Immediately after the show completed production, Joey asked Amy out. They continued to date steadily.

OUR THIRTIETH WEDDING ANNIVERSARY

August 25, 2009, marked my and Joanne's thirtieth wedding anniversary. We couldn't believe how fast time was moving. We discussed how to celebrate this milestone of thirty wonderful years. We booked an ocean-view room and a night at the beautiful David Geffen Hotel in Malibu. She arranged for a private dining room, and we hosted a small dinner party. It was perfect—thirty years and still in love. We discussed the cycle of life, and we were hopeful that we would soon dance at Scott's and Amy's weddings and later experience the joy of being grandparents. As for the Amy and Joey romance, it seemed to be heating up.

Amy had great taste in style and fashion, areas in which I was woefully lacking. So I asked "my consultant" to help me find something nice for Mom. The week before the anniversary party, Amy accompanied me to XIV Karats, a jewelry store on Beverly Drive in Beverly Hills. It seems like yesterday. Amy had great familiarity with the store and the inventory, and she even found a salesperson with whom she and Joanne were familiar. Amy was charming and so beautiful. I watched her take charge in a graceful manner. How truly blessed I was, although I have to admit that the feeling dissipated a little when I saw the bill. The shock, of course, was only short lived.

In March 2010, we joyfully attended and celebrated the bar mitzvah of Jacob Blum, the son of our dear friend Monique Blum. As a matter of background, Joanne first met Monique when Jacob was a student in Joanne's third-grade class at Abraham Heschel Day School in Northridge. It was the first week of school, and it was just before class commenced when an attractive and charming, youthful blond woman approached Joanne.

She introduced herself as Monique Blum, the mother of Jacob. She explained that Jacob was very tall for his age and was frequently placed in the back of his classroom because of his height. This tended to interfere with his ability to concentrate in class. Joanne looked at Monique and was struck by the manner in which she reminded her so much of herself when Scott was in the third grade and she had approached Scott's teacher. Jacob moved to the front row, and an unbelievably special friendship ensued.

Over the next five or six years, Monique, Jake, and Monique's fiancé, Joe, became like family. We went on vacations together and spent every weekend together. Joanne and Monique were kindred spirits. They mostly laughed together and unfortunately sometimes cried together. In the tough times, they held each other up. It's rare in life to have the connection and the love that these two shared.

At the Four Seasons Hotel bar mitzvah cocktail hour, I was approached by Joey Port. He told me how Amy was the most wonderful woman he had ever met in his life, and he had never been happier. He said he was in love. You really didn't have to be a rocket scientist to see where this conversation was headed. Then, all of a sudden, Joey changed gears on me. "Neil," he said, "I know how much you like coffee. There's a café near my house called Kings Road. They brew the best coffee in Los Angeles." I tried figuring out how this conversation transitioned so quickly from love to coffee. Joey then said, "Can I come by your hotel room tomorrow morning and bring you and Joanne some coffee?" "Great," I responded, "Looking forward to it."

The party was spectacular. Joanne and I stayed up late with Monique, recapping the evening, and retired to our hotel room at two-thirty or three in the morning. At about 7:30 a.m. the next morning (Sunday), we were sound asleep when we were awakened by repeated knocking on the door. We both woke up, and Joanne looked at me in amazement. "Who could that be this early?" I went to the door and asked, "Who is it?" The knocker responded, "It's Joey." Joanne immediately fled to the bathroom to change from her nightgown.

I opened the door and greeted Joey, who said, "I hope I'm not here too early. Where's Joanne?" "She's in the bathroom, Joey." "Well, I brought you both coffee from Kings Road." I thought to myself, *This stuff better be good.* Joanne soon emerged from the bathroom, still in a state of amazement.

Joey then said, "I'm sure you know I just didn't come here to bring you coffee. I told Neil last night how special Amy is and how much I love her. I'd like your permission to marry her." Joanne's jaw dropped, and I waited a moment for her to regain her composure. Since Joanne was speechless, I responded on her behalf, "You have our permission, Joey, if Amy's on board." It was a great moment. Joey was a wonderful guy from a great family. Within twenty-four hours, they were engaged. Joanne and I were ecstatic and began to explore wedding venues. We couldn't stop talking about our good fortune. Plans were preliminarily made to book the Hotel Casa del Mar in Santa Monica for August of 2011.

Soon Joey's parents, Phyllis and Steve Port, flew out from Altoona, Pennsylvania. They were lovely people, and we bonded immediately. The six of us had lunch at the Hotel Casa del Mar. After lunch, we walked on the boardwalk in Santa Monica. All we could see was the beauty of the Pacific Ocean, blue skies, and sunshine brightening our future.

Storm on the Horizon

Amy was not only now engaged, but she had also made a career change. Frustrated and disillusioned with the television industry, she took an interim job teaching preschool until she figured out the direction of her life. She was considering going back to school to obtain a master's degree.

Instead, Amy took a teaching position as an early childhood educator at Pressman Academy in Los Angeles. What was initially intended as a space-filler until she could figure out what she wanted to do with the rest of her life unexpectedly evolved into a great passion. Amy fell in love with her position at Pressman.

While teaching sometime in the latter part of April 2010, Amy developed what appeared to be a viral illness manifesting itself in a cough, congestion, and a low-grade temperature. As a preschool teacher, she was constantly exposed to runny noses. About a year earlier, she had another respiratory infection that was diagnosed as walking pneumonia. It eventually cleared up and went away. Accompanying the apparent viral illness of

April 2010 was severe right rib pain. She went to an urgent care center, where she was diagnosed as having a musculoskeletal strain of the rib cage. With all the coughing she was doing, the diagnosis made perfect sense. She was advised to take anti-inflammatory medication. Instead, she sought out an acupuncturist without any benefit and then was referred by a friend to a chiropractor. The chiropractor said that the ribs appeared to be properly aligned and that her condition warranted an internal medicine evaluation rather than chiropractic treatment.

In the meantime, Amy was feeling progressively fatigued to the point where it was difficult to carry out her normal teaching activities at school. Her energy level was being drained, and she started to experience a lack of appetite. Joanne then took her to an internist for a chest X-ray, which confirmed the presence of a very large effusion involving the right middle and right lower lobes of the right lung. The internist hospitalized Amy. Her cough was now chronic and heavy.

A CAT scan was performed in the hospital the morning after her admission. The CAT scan revealed that the right lung was almost entirely collapsed. The doctor had initially speculated that Amy had pulmonary emboli. However, the scan revealed a ten-millimeter nodule in the hepatic lobe that the doctors felt was possibly a hemangioma. Amy was immediately placed on a myriad of antibiotics administered through an IV line. A biopsy was ordered to test the sheath of fluid that was covering her chest. The fluid had such depth and force that it caused her right lung to submerge. Now collapsed, it significantly impaired her breathing capacity.

A pulmonologist was called into the case. He was very stoic. His eyes were light blue, his hair white, and his skin pale. He looked around the hospital room. He asked me who I was, he asked Joanne who she was, and he asked our friend Monique who she was. He appeared to be detached and perhaps had knowledge or a premonition of the potentially grave nature of Amy's condition. He said it would take a few days to get the results back, and he would be out of town for the rest of Memorial Day weekend. Amy was released, and, with mounting tension, the entire family awaited the Monday morning phone call with the results of the pathology results.

The call never came despite Joanne tenaciously calling on an hourly basis, begging for the process to be expedited. I was at work, but my mind was at home. I called Joanne repeatedly, and she told me to stop calling, stating that when she heard something I would be the first to know. I came home that night, and there was still no news.

On Tuesday morning, I received a phone call at the office. The voice was not that of Joanne but rather Amy. Matter-of-factly, she said, "Dad, I have cancer." It was couched in such a way that her disbelief was apparent. Had she really fallen victim to this dreaded disease, or were we all experiencing a bad dream? I was at a loss for words. How could I tell my only precious daughter not to worry when I was struggling to not drown in the face of fear? "Amy," I said, "they have great drugs now to fight cancer. You're a fighter; we'll beat this." There was no response on her end. After a moment of silence, she said, "Here's Mom, Dad." In a state of panic, Joanne hurriedly said she had doctors to call and abruptly hung up. She then returned my call, indicating that she had an appointment for Amy the following morning with a thoracic surgeon. Joanne said that he was the same thoracic surgeon who had operated on legendary Lakers announcer Chick Hearn.

The night before the consult, Amy spiked a fever. It was a raging fever of 104. She was immediately admitted that evening to Northridge Hospital, where antibiotics were administered through an IV.

The following morning, the thoracic surgeon took a biopsy of the lung and tried to re-inflate the right lung. Prior to being wheeled down to the operating room, Amy looked at me fearfully and in her soft gentle voice said, "Daddy..." She grabbed my hand. "Am I going to die?" She then began to chant the Hebrew prayer "Modeh Ani" as she was wheeled into surgery. This sudden display of religious practice was surprising as Amy wasn't an observant Jew. The "Modeh Ani" prayer is recited each morning upon awakening by an observant Jew. Though not an observant Jew herself, Amy was now being exposed in her work at the Pressman Academy to a world of faith and religion. The translation of the prayer is, "I offer thanks before You, Living and Eternal King, for You mercifully restored my soul within me; Your faithfulness is great." As she was wheeled into surgery, I, too, prayed for divine intervention and the restoration of both Amy's soul and good health.

Joanne and I nervously waited in the surgical reception room. An eternity seemed to have passed when finally the surgeon came out in his surgical gown, slowly removing his mask, his face lacking emotion and optimism. He stared into our eyes and regrettably said he couldn't inflate the lung. There was a sheath covering her entire chest full of cancer cells that had invaded the chest wall cavity. The right lung was now collapsed and submerged under the fluid. He told us that he believed that the cancer had now spread well into the lymph nodes. It was conjectural as to whether or not it had spread to any organs other than the right lung. He said the cancer probably originated elsewhere in Amy's body, but he couldn't say where. "She's a twenty-six-year-old female nonsmoker with no toxic exposure. This is both tragic and puzzling," he said.

Amy was fever-free that afternoon and remained in Northridge Hospital that night. Joanne slept in the room with her. I stayed until 1:00 a.m. then went home to try to sleep, returning six hours later. The oncologist was scheduled to meet us at the hospital that morning. Prior to our meeting with the oncologist, our friend Michael and his wife, Janice, came to the hospital. Michael is a physician and cancer survivor and, per Joanne's request, graciously agreed to talk with the oncologist.

We intercepted the oncologist before he went into Amy's room. The oncologist immediately unfolded the worst-case scenario. He told me, "Your daughter is a very sick girl with a very bad prognosis." He then stated that the odds are against her. Michael revealed his own history, saying that he was once a statistic that doctors said would die five years ago. Today he was in remission, working again and, whenever possible, nurturing and counseling other cancer patients. He then rendered a caveat to the oncologist: "Don't discuss statistics with that young girl. Don't break her spirit."

The oncologist stared at Michael, speechless. He looked downward at the floor as his glasses were wavering on the tip of his nose and appeared to be in danger of descending all the way to the floor. He suddenly jerked his body upward, removed himself from the uncomfortable chair that he was seated in and, in a marching-like manner, without responding to Michael, proceeded to Amy's hospital room. We followed suit. Would he listen to Michael's advice?

The oncologist spoke in a strong Eastern European accent. He wore bifocals that constantly slid to the tip of his nose. He constantly waved his arms as if he were a bird trying to fly. As a matter of fact, he seemed to speak with his arms and hands as opposed to with his mouth. Doom was the expression painted on his face.

Upon entering Amy's hospital room, the oncologist introduced himself. Rather than asking how she was feeling, he immediately said, "I have grim news for you. You have cancer." Amy looked at him with a sense of amusement on her face: perhaps it was the glasses straddling the edge of his nose, about to fall off, perhaps it was his oversized suit, or perhaps it was the constant movement of his arms.

Amy responded, "Doctor, I already know that I have cancer." She then asked the question we all were wondering, "Am I going to die soon?" The doctor threw his hands up in the air; his eyes were spinning. "Die!" he said. "We're all going to die. I can't tell you when you'll die." He then quickly changed the subject. "I'm going to put you on a drug; I'm not certain this is the right drug, but I think it might be the right drug. We won't know if it's the right drug until the pathology reports come back from UCLA and other laboratories in about six weeks. At that time we'll have a more definitive idea of what the treatment protocol should be, but we'll start you on this drug right now because I think it might work." The drug was Tarceva.

Two days later, Amy was released from the hospital, still running a slight fever just under a hundred. The fluid was continuing to build up in her chest wall cavity. A catheter was surgically inserted to drain it. Her oncologist gave us three Tarceva pills. He explained in his thick accent that they were having problems getting the approval of the insurance company. "Today is Friday," he told me. "Let's meet late Sunday afternoon at Northridge Hospital, at which time I will give you three more pills." He then went on a tirade against the FDA. Joanne asked whether the Mayo Clinic, City of Hope, or the Anderson Cancer Institute at the University of Texas might offer us hope. The doctor raised his arms and said, "I don't know. They don't know any more than we do. This is an unusual cancer of unknown origin." He speculated that the origin might be the pancreas, but more conclusive testing and data needed to be obtained.

That Sunday, I met the oncologist late in the afternoon at Northridge Hospital. He had a small bag with three Tarceva pills in it. It almost seemed like it was a clandestine meeting with the KGB or a drug deal. I felt that this was less than professional and certainly awkward. But we, like so many others, were at the mercy of insurance companies and the limitations of modern medicine. Nevertheless, at that moment, this was all that we had: three Tarceva pills and hope.

At this point you're probably wondering why we selected this oncologist. I had carried Amy on my group health insurance up until the age of twenty-five. It's an outstanding PPO plan with access to the best doctors in the city. Unfortunately, after twenty-five, the coverage ceased. Amy was now over twenty-five and working. Unbeknownst to me, she had an option at her job to either select HMO coverage with no financial contribution to premiums on her end or to choose the PPO option, which meant she would contribute to the premiums. Up until that time Amy had always been relatively healthy; she opted for the HMO plan. She was stuck with the HMO until October 1, 2010, at which time there would be open enrollment, and she could switch into the PPO. So, until October 1, 2010, we had to keep Amy alive in the HMO system. Dr. Michael indicated that after several discussions with the oncologist, despite his social fumbling and bumbling, he felt he was a good doctor. Michael also said that Tarceva was a good drug. He was on it himself for a while. The key was whether or not Amy's genetic mutation would respond to it.

At the KGB-like meeting at Northridge Hospital, I took the opportunity to have a candid discussion with the doctor. I asked him, "Honestly, what is my daughter's life expectancy?" Again, the grim reaper spoke. "She has an aggressive form of lung cancer," he said. "The prognosis is bad. I would give her about three months to live."

It was June 2010. I once again reminded the doctor never to mention statistics to my daughter or wife. Amy's fighting spirit could not be dampened. The doctor looked at me almost teary-eyed and said, "I understand."

Meanwhile, Joanne had other ideas concerning the management of Amy's medical care. She made arrangements for a prominent oncologist to shadow the HMO oncologist. We paid him out of pocket. We had all of the records from the HMO sent to the private oncologist, who reviewed everything and monitored the plan of action of the HMO physicians. He agreed with them and said they were exercising the standard of care in the community. Meanwhile, Amy's breathing became more labored, and the fluid buildup increased. The constant discomfort of a catheter in her chest made it impossible for her to sleep on her stomach.

Joanne's heart was breaking; she couldn't stand to see Amy suffer. She did extensive research, which led her to a thoracic surgeon at a prominent hospital in Los Angeles. We had an appointment on Monday, June 21, 2010, to meet with this renowned thoracic surgeon. The word was he was the best. Joanne hoped he could perform a surgical procedure and stop the fluid buildup. He charged five hundred dollars up front. The consultation was five or possibly ten minutes at the most. After the consultation, he said he had nothing to offer us.

But, the following day, our spirits were somewhat lifted. We received news from the HMO that the results of a recently administered CT scan showed that Amy's liver and pancreas as of June 22, 2010, were clean, with no sign of cancer. Also the pathology test and tumor markers for breast cancer were normal. That was the only good news we had received in a while.

On June 23, 2010, we met with the HMO oncologist at eight-thirty in the morning. Once again, the two people Joanne now called her "angels," Dr. Michael and his wife, Janice, met us at the appointment. The oncologist advised us that they still couldn't determine the primary source of the cancer. The pathology reports were slow in coming back. Tumor markers in the liver and pancreas were elevated, but he couldn't state whether that was the source. Again, he emphasized the unusual nature of the cancer. He also added that the prognosis was not good. For the first time, the doctor had slipped. I looked at Amy's face; she looked frozen and emotionless. The oncologist said that Amy could stay on the Tarceva drug "another week or two, and we'll see how she responds." They would monitor the fluid. If the fluid lessened, that would mean the Tarceva was working. If the fluid didn't ease up then they would investigate other options. Other options included various types of chemotherapy that had major side effects and risks.

The Tarceva that Amy was taking had a side effect of acne. Her beautiful skin had suddenly erupted into a plane of acne sores and puss. In the middle of the doctor's presentation explaining the risk factors of the chemotherapy, Amy interrupted him and asked if she could freeze her eggs. The oncologist stared at her, speechless, and then stated, "This would involve a surgical procedure that I wouldn't recommend at this time." Joanne then asked the doctor if chemotherapy would destroy her eggs or if she could get pregnant in the future. The oncologist paused, his eyes like steel, his body stiff, his arms now still, and said, "Let's not talk about the future." He then added, "Pregnancy would put both Amy and a baby at risk." He quickly changed the subject and said, "I'm going on vacation for a week. I will return after July fourth."

That Saturday, Amy spent the day at Joey's house. She was always upbeat when she was there. On Sunday, June 27, 2010, Amy's UC Santa Barbara roommate, Jenny, visited from Orange County. A lovely young lady, Jenny was now a special education teacher. It was a pleasure to see her. Her perky spirit was uplifting for Amy. They spent the day together, laughing and reminiscing.

Amy's brief optimism was deflated when a home healthcare nurse removed 700 cc of fluid from her lung that night. The home healthcare nurse was coming every three days to remove the fluid, which appeared to be building up, indicative of the fact that the Tarceva might not be working. That evening, the three of us and Amy's friend Jenny went to Monique's house for dinner and had an enjoyable time, escaping briefly our grim reality. We returned home then Jenny kissed Amy good-bye and drove back to Orange County.

After Jenny left, Amy wouldn't talk to us. She went into her bedroom and shut the door. Joanne attempted to walk in, but Amy snapped at her and told her to leave her alone and get out of her room. Joanne returned to our bedroom, trembling and in tears. "I can't go on like this. I don't want to live. It's only going to get worse. What are we going to do? We are living in hell." I put my arms around Joanne. I knew there were no words to comfort her. We were now truly a family in crisis. As she cried, I held back my own tears. I thought about how quickly lives can change. I thought about the coming challenge of holding my family together. And I looked at the broken soul of my wife, once the source of strength for others, now grasping for the inner strength to hold on.

On Monday, June 29, 2010, Joanne visited her friend Monica (not Monique). Monica had two daughters—one was a year younger than Amy; one was a year older. They were good friends during elementary and middle school. They spent much time together, both the girls and their mothers. Monica told Joanne about her aunt who was battling cancer. She was being treated at the Anderson Center in Texas. Monica said miracles were being performed there. Joanne called me at work and said that we had to go to Texas immediately. I checked out their website and discovered that if you sent your medical file, they would respond and render an opinion as to whether they might be helpful with a treatment modality. Joanne ordered all of Amy's records and sent them off to Anderson. In the interim, she heard about a doctor who was affiliated with a major hospital in Los Angeles. His reputation was topnotch. An appointment was set for July 1, 2010, the day after our appointment with our HMO.

Our HMO oncologist was on vacation until after July 4, 2010. We saw his associate, a warm Indian woman approximately forty years old. She had lots of bedside manner. She looked compassionately into our eyes and said, "You know this is a very tough kind of cancer, extremely unusual. My advice is to live each day to its fullest. We will know by the end of the week if the Tarceva is working. If the Tarceva isn't working, we will start an aggressive chemotherapy regimen."

She said Amy would probably lose her hair, her eyelashes, and her eyebrows, and added, "Other potential risks include infection and blood clots." The doctor also indicated that Amy wasn't compatible with the platinum component of therapy. "She will have to do without it or a substitute will have to be found."

Upon our arrival home, Amy's mood was amazing. Despite the grim news, she had a smile on her face and called Joey. They were on the phone and laughed the night away. She appeared to have adhered to the doctor's advice to live each day to the fullest.

The next day, we visited Dr. Hess. He was quite impressive—bright and articulate—and spoke with clarity. He was the first physician who was optimistic and gave us hope. He explained to us that Amy had built up a great deal of scar tissue in her chest. This was good because it created a barricade to contain the cancer from spreading. He told us that the pain Amy was experiencing in her shoulder was the lung trying to expand. Finally, he indicated that she might be a candidate for clinical trial drugs. He asked for pathology reports and indicated that he would try to match her genetic mutation. It was an outstanding day.

Unfortunately, that Friday, July 2, was as bad as that Thursday, July 1, was good. A friend called Amy and asked her what stage of cancer she had. For some reason, possibly denial, Amy thought she was in stage three, and when Joanne advised her that she was in stage four, Amy sunk into a deep depression, closed her door, and slept the entire day.

While Amy was sleeping, the HMO called and instructed Joanne to have Amy stop the Tarceva. The drug wasn't working. Almost concurrently, Joanne received a phone call from Dr. Hess's office cautioning us not to start chemotherapy until they heard from UCLA with the ALK results next week. Joanne called me at the office, upset. She brought me up to speed and said she was losing faith in all the doctors. She had several calls that day. The ex-principal of her school suggested that she see a leading oncologist in Encino. Her friend Monica continued to urge her to take Amy to Texas to the Anderson Cancer Clinic. Another friend directed us to the Mayo Clinic and yet another to the Sloan Kettering Center. Joanne was ready to go anywhere to cure our daughter.

By Saturday, July 3, 2010, Amy had stopped the Tarceva. The side effects, of which we had been warned, were apparent. Amy had terrible acne on her face. She had mouth sores that were horrible; it was difficult and painful for her to eat and swallow. She was in bed all that day, depressed and in discomfort. The medication Tarceva left her with only acne and mouth sores and had no appreciable effect on the cancer. Not only did the Tarceva not work, but Amy felt worse, both physically and emotionally. The home healthcare nurse came and drained 700 cc of fluid from her chest.

I spent that morning in line at the Department of Motor Vehicles. Someone stole Joanne's registration sticker off her license plate. After she had been a victim of theft, the police department added insult to injury by pulling her over and giving her a ticket for not having a registration sticker on her license plate. I paid the Department of Motor Vehicles for a new registration tag; something that might have previously angered me was now inconsequential.

⋅➤═◉═◀⋅

The Hotel Casa del Mar in Santa Monica was the scheduled venue for Amy and Joey's August 2011 wedding. As we now approached July 4, 2010, it was apparent that the best-made plans can fall victim to the hand of fate. We didn't know if Amy would even be with us in August 2011, so Joanne suggested that we spend two nights on the Fourth of July weekend at the Hotel Casa del Mar. She booked one room for Joey and Amy and one room for us. Joanne sadly looked into my eyes and said, "After all, Neil, Amy may not be with us the next

Fourth of July." And so it was a joyous weekend at the beach, a Fourth of July weekend we would never forget. Amy was physically weakened, but her spirits ran high. She amazingly lit up rooms with her beautiful smile and gentle spirit.

Amy was now well into her chemotherapy, and her hair was rapidly falling out. On July 6, she and Joanne went wig shopping and bought two beautiful wigs. July also marked the beginning of frequent hospitalizations for as long as seven days at a time. These hospitalizations were necessitated by infections, including staph, which raged like a wildfire, almost killing Amy. There were numerous bouts of dehydration. All the while Amy remained courageous; despite being beaten up, she postured herself on the side of optimism and courage and continued to hope for the silver-bullet clinical trial drug. While she hoped, it was becoming apparent to me that what we needed was a miracle. The scenario played itself out over several months. It was a rollercoaster ride of tolerable and less tolerable periods.

The Nurse Who Wouldn't Leave

As I mentioned, a home healthcare nurse would come to the house daily to drain the fluid building up in Amy's chest. The procedure usually took about twenty minutes, and the nurse was in and out in no time. The agency would send different nurses, but periodically we would see a familiar face. They were all pleasant and professional. However, there is always the exception. In this case it started one night upon my coming home from work. I noticed a late-model Honda Civic. It looked like it had logged enough miles to max out the odometer. Between the discoloration of the car's paint and the dirt buildup, the color of the car was undeterminable. There were enough visible dents to lead the observer to conclude it belonged to a bad driver or at least a person possessed with bad luck, or both.

Upon entering our house, I walked into Amy's bedroom. The room was pink and decorated with some of her artwork. She was a gifted artist. It was under these circumstances that I first met Nurse Peggy. In her mid-fifties, she had very short, curly, oily, brownish-red hair and a ruddy complexion. Peggy was appropriately dressed in a typical white nurses' uniform, albeit wrinkled, stained, and in desperate need of cleaning. My first impression was concern. She appeared to have completed draining Amy's chest and, with a strong Boston accent, was chatting nonstop.

Joanne managed to muzzle her just long enough to offer an introduction. Peggy acknowledged me with the nod of her head and a quick, "Nice to meet you. I love your wife and daughter." She then jumped back into her monologue, informing us that she had been a private nurse for some of Hollywood's biggest names. I found her annoying, but Joanne and Amy displayed a sense of being both entertained and distracted from the grim reality of the moment.

Joanne invited Peggy to join us in the kitchen for dinner, and, without hesitation, she accepted. While seated, I heard our dog, Scruffy, barking in the backyard. As I listened more carefully, I heard that there were actually two dogs barking angrily. To fill you in, we adopted Scruffy as a rescue about nine years earlier. He was a Boston terrier, a little of this, and a little of that. Get the picture? He was nothing to look at, resembling a well-used Brillo pad, but he had a good and gentle soul. Despite being a little territorial, Scruffy was very good-natured and was prone to minding his own business. Amy was much more connected to Joey's dog, Rooney, than to Scruffy. Joanne, however, was crazy about Scruffy. She spent countless hours running him to veterinarians and veterinary specialists for his heart condition, asthma, arthritis, and a neurological condition frequently resulting in seizures.

Joanne became alarmed when she heard the canine uprising. We quickly proceeded to the backyard, where the two dogs were nose to nose and toe to toe. Joanne stepped between them and retrieved Scruffy, averting his going into a seizure or having a heart attack. She brought him back into the house, where, at last, there was peace.

Peggy talked incessantly, relating one miraculous cancer story after another. It sounded as if the stories were right out of the *The National Enquirer* or another supermarket tabloid. But Joanne's eyes were open wide. This is what she wanted to hear. Peggy was wearing on me, and all I could hear was the voice of doctors: the HMO oncologist with his grim prognosis, the Indian HMO oncologist who said this is a tough and unusual cancer and to "enjoy every minute." I also recall the silence and stoic stare of the first pulmonologist who examined Amy in the hospital. Foremost, I saw the suffering of my daughter and my inability to stop it. I clearly had enough of Peggy, excused myself, and headed for Amy's bedroom. She was now in bed with her laptop, busy on Facebook. She looked up and smiled, blew me a kiss, and said, "Goodnight, Dad." I got the picture; she wanted her space. I called my brother and chatted for a while, followed by a shower. I was now hopeful that Peggy the Nurse was gone.

As I approached the den, I heard the television and Peggy's booming Bostonian voice. I walked in, struggling to be friendly, and told Joanne I was retiring for the night. Joanne proceeded to advise me that Peggy was going to sleep over in our extra bedroom. She added, "Peggy has an old car with a lot of mechanical problems. She lives in a bad part of town and is afraid to drive her car there this late." I thought to myself, *Why didn't she anticipate the problem a few hours ago?* I kissed Joanne good-night, perturbed that my emotionally vulnerable wife just got duped by one of life's many manipulative con artists, just what we needed in our lives at this time. But what bothered me even more was the possibility that this stranger was now giving Joanne the emotional strength I couldn't provide. And on that unsettling note, I retired for the night.

The following day, I was ecstatic to arrive home from work with no sign of Peggy's car. Upon entering our house, I was greeted by Joanne. I asked about Amy and whether a nurse had drained her yet. This procedure was usually performed before 5:00 p.m. Joanne proceeded to say, "Peggy called, and she is running late, but she should be here by eight. I can tell that you don't like her, but she's knowledgeable, and she is really interested in helping us. She asked me to call the agency and have her assigned to us every day. It's so much better to have the same nurse come daily." "Joanne, if that's what you want, fine. I personally find her unprofessional, but we have bigger issues so whatever."

At nine-thirty, Peggy rang our doorbell. She held her dog with a leash in one hand and a large duffle bag in the other. As the washing machine and dryer worked late into the night, I learned from Joanne the next day about poor Peggy's laundry woes, home foreclosure, and bankruptcy. And, yes, she once again slept at our house. Several days passed, and Amy was also on to Peggy. "This lady is taking advantage of Mom's vulnerable state," she said. "I think we need to talk to Mom." Peggy helped the process the following day. She left our house in the morning and said she would return at six in the evening to drain Amy's chest. Six came and went and no Peggy. Seven and no Peggy. Joanne insisted that Peggy would show up momentarily. I suggested that we call the agency to send out another nurse. Joanne agreed, but she was now fearful that something had happened to Peggy. "Joanne, we are placing Amy at risk," I said. The agency sent out another nurse, and Amy was drained and fell asleep.

At nine-thirty, Peggy called. She told Joanne that she stopped at Target to do a little shopping. She lost track of both time and her car keys and was locked out of her automobile. Joanne asked her if she was a member of the Auto Club Road Service. "No," she responded. "Stay put. I'll be there in a few minutes and call the Auto Club." I tried to persuade Joanne to let me handle it and meet Peggy. She declined, telling me to watch Amy, and she was quickly out the door. They both returned about an hour later. Joanne looked exhausted. Peggy looked hungry as she opened our refrigerator and proclaimed, "I could eat a horse." The Peggy situation was out of control but soon would be abated. Amy had a raging temperature the next day. This necessitated another hospitalization at Northridge Hospital.

When Amy was released, she told us that Peggy had outworn her stay and was increasingly becoming both a nuisance and a burden. We requested that the agency not assign her anymore. We also asked them to refrain from telling her the truth. Peggy called a few times, somewhat angry with the agency for telling her that she wasn't working for us any longer due to travel considerations. Peggy even called Joanne and asked that she intervene. Joanne said she would see what she could do. Soon thereafter, the calls from Peggy ended.

Yom Kippur
(2010)

Sundown on Friday, September 17, 2010, marked the beginning of the holiest day of the Jewish calendar, Yom Kippur. Yom Kippur is a twenty-four-hour day of atonement and repentance that consists of attending synagogue, fasting, and intensive prayer. It is said that G-d inscribes each person's fate for the coming year on Rosh Hashanah. On Yom Kippur, the verdict is sealed. Who shall live? And who shall die? These words are chanted repeatedly throughout the services. Recited during the service is the prayer entitled "U Netaneh Tokef." Throughout my entire life, the prayer has had a haunting and chilling effect upon me. The words "who will live and who will die?" were particularly disturbing this Yom Kippur.

I attended Yom Kippur services with Joanne, Amy, Joey, and Scott at Temple Beth Am, which housed the Pressman Academy, where Amy taught. It was a source of inspiration and strength for Amy. As we sat together during the service, I looked at my family. Scott was seated to my right. Joanne was seated to my left. Amy sat next to her. And Joey sat to the left of Amy. When the "Unaetaneh Tokef" prayer ("Let Us Tell How Utterly Holy This Day Is") was chanted, I turned my head to the left to look at my daughter. On her exterior, she was poised and courageous, perhaps the strongest of the five of us seated there. Joanne squeezed my hand. She then turned to the right, whispering in my ear, "Can you see my tears?" "Only two or three," I said. She tried to avoid eye contact with Amy. While we both knew it was likely that this was Amy's last Yom Kippur, no one would ever imagine that it would be Joanne's.

⋄⟹◉⟸⋄

Finally, in October 2010, we switched oncologists. Good-bye to the grim reaper and now on to a new set of eyes, Dr. Brown's. The styles of the two physicians were strikingly different: the former scientifically stoic and blunt, the latter cautiously optimistic, warm, and embracing.

The disease process continued to hasten, now affecting both its victim, Amy as well as Joanne. Joanne was now worn down both physically and emotionally. She cried every night. She was so worried about Amy that she failed to take care of herself. She couldn't remember whether she had taken her hypertension medication, and at times I wondered if she even cared. The clock continued to tick. Amy's condition was slowly worsening.

Joanne arranged for a consultation with the City of Hope in Duarte, California. Dr. Michael accompanied us. We met with a physician who had reviewed Amy's file. She once again advised us that Amy had a very unusual form of lung cancer. There was one possible clinical trial drug that might be beneficial; however, it had realized more success with ovarian cancer and had not yet been tested for lung cancer. She suggested that we stick with the conventional chemotherapy, and her team would continue to monitor incoming drugs. And so it was several more months of chemotherapy for Amy.

On Friday, April 1, 2011, Joanne and Amy had an appointment at the University of California, Irvine Medical Center. We desperately were seeking a clinical trial drug as a backup to conventional chemotherapy. Amy and Joanne met with an oncologist at the medical center, and after the usual and customary tedious exercise of filling out forms, including medical history, they met with the oncologist. They hoped that this oncologist might hold the key to Amy's life via a potent clinical trial drug.

Upon completion of the meeting, Joanne called me on her cell phone. She sounded tired and depressed. She advised me that the meeting offered no help. The doctor told them that the odds weren't favorable that Amy would qualify for a clinical study. Furthermore, he needed to study additional slides from her recently performed liver biopsy. He explained that if they could secure a more defined clarification of her genetic mutation, it might enhance the prospect of her being accepted into a trial. Too many ifs and not enough hope.

Broadsided by the Hand of Fate

That night we were alone as Amy decided to spend the weekend at Joey's. Joanne and I would spend every Friday night at the home of Monique and her fiancé, Joe. But tonight was different. Joanne complained of a bad headache and dizziness. She thought she might have a little virus. I reminded her that she had had the headache and dizziness for about two days. She insisted that it was nothing serious and that she would take some Advil. She canceled dinner with Monique, which was a rarity. I brought some takeout food in for dinner. As we ate, Joanne cried. "She's going to die…" With rhythmic progressions, she continued hysterically, "She's going to die, I know it. There's nothing else they can do for her."

After dinner, Joanne took a warm bath, and, after an exhausting day, we both retired to bed early. She had a special radiance and glow about her that night. She was always beautiful, but on that night she was extraordinarily beautiful. I looked into her soulful brown eyes and thought how lucky I was to have her to travel the rugged terrain of this most difficult journey with. I felt a burning love deep within and an appreciation of my soul mate and anchor for thirty-two years. As we got into bed, we embraced, and Joanne cried a steady flow of tears. Her fire of hope had been extinguished.

Joanne wore a sleeveless light-yellow nightgown to bed. It was her favorite. She set her alarm clock early because she was planning to meet Monique for an early exercise class. Early Saturday morning, the alarm clock burst with the vibration of a new day. Usually a light sleeper and easily awakened, Joanne slept through the alarm. "Jo," I said, "turn off the alarm...turn off your alarm." Finally, I arose, walked to her side of the bed, and turned off the alarm. I then looked at her and said, "Jo?" She appeared lifeless. I tried to shake her, but I couldn't awaken her. I immediately called 911. They instructed me to administer CPR, but her mouth was locked tight. It wouldn't move. I started compressing her chest as the 911 operator instructed me. She was lying on her side. I felt her hands; they were ice cold and locked tight. It was clear to me that she was dead. I couldn't believe it. They arrived on the scene shortly thereafter. The paramedics checked her vital signs. All I can remember from the time I tried to resuscitate her was asking why. "Why now? You can't leave me, Joanne, not now after thirty-two years. I need you. Please don't leave me here. This must be a nightmare. Please don't go; don't leave me here alone."

I telephoned my brother and sister to tell them what had happened. My sister said she would contact Amy and Scott and would be over shortly.

The mortuary was contacted to pick up her body. I stared at the woman I loved, but it was no longer Joanne. It was merely an empty vessel. Joanne had died of a broken heart, manifesting itself physically by way of cardiopulmonary arrest, secondary to a cerebral vascular accident. I strongly felt her absence, her soul unleashed into a new dimension, her existence now suspended from mine, from Amy's, from Scott's, and from the physical world. My life was now shattered, my consciousness numbed in disbelief. What had happened to the world as I once knew it? How would Scott and Amy cope with this profound loss and change of circumstance? I raised my hands to the sky and shouted, "Please tell me this is a bad dream. Why? Why?"

Soon I was joined by Amy, who had been at Joey's; Scott; my brother, Randy; my sister, Leslie; my brother-in-law, Dan; and our friend Monique. We stared blankly at each other in utter disbelief. Time stood still. We were all reminded that life is but a narrow and fragile bridge.

Sunday April 3, 2011: I was accompanied to Mount Sinai Funeral Home by my brother, Randy. We had made this trek before, making funeral arrangements for our parents. Randy had stood by my side through every crisis in my life. This was clearly the biggest. We made funeral arrangements and selected a casket. I was asked if I desired a *Shomer*. Joanne had once told me that if she died before me, she wanted a *Shomer*. In Jewish tradition, the *Shomer* watches the body at all times until buried, protecting it from evil spirits. Psalms are read during this time.

Joanne's funeral was conducted on April 4, 2011, at Mount Sinai in Simi Valley. Rabbi Jerry Cutler of the Temple of the Creative Arts officiated. Rabbi Cutler had married my sister, Leslie, and brother-in-law, Dan. The Rabbi's daughter was a classmate of Amy's at Heschel Day School. He had recently officiated at the funeral of actress Elizabeth Taylor. He knew Joanne from the Heschel community. There was a strong connection.

Emotional eulogies were delivered by Scott, Amy, Leslie, and Lara Martin. I also gave a eulogy, but none were more touching than those of Scott and Amy. Amy told me that she didn't have the physical or emotional strength to give a eulogy. The morning of the funeral, she approached me. "Dad," she said, "I've changed my mind. I want to give a eulogy." And when her turn came, she courageously stepped up to the microphone, fighting off the tears and emotion. She then shared what everyone already knew, her deep love and admiration for her mother, Joanne.

Now it was Scott's turn to eulogize his mother. I will never forget the picture he painted of his deep love for her and how she forever touched his life.

SCOTT'S EULOGY FOR HIS MOTHER

I initially balked at the opportunity of delivering a eulogy this afternoon. Like my mother, I can be emotional, which could result in more tears than words. I was also daunted that my remarks might amount to no more than lofty, hackneyed phrases, which would reflect poorly on me, bore you, and certainly fail to articulate the reverence and veneration that

I hold for my mother. With that said, my intention here today is to share a brief glimpse into the life of my mother, which is comprised of more words and details than tears and banalities.

My mother didn't live a life that lent itself to a snarky eulogy, with funny stories about her telling off her boss or comments to me like, "Life's hard; get used to it." For those of you who knew my mother, I am sure you can appreciate my difficulty in crafting a eulogy that isn't chockfull of certain overused descriptions and phrases in the world of eulogies. So, kindly bear with me as I try to interject some originality into the following thoughts about a woman who lived a life that genuinely embodied those bromidic sermons that we sometimes hear about individuals who are no longer with us.

Before I continue, please accept the gratitude my family bestows upon each of you who has come to pay your respects to my beloved mother, with special veneration to those of you who hopped on planes with less than twenty-four hours' notice to console our family and witness my mother's spirit gracefully rise to the heavens.

Most of you knew my mother well, but please allow me to summarize the woman we are here to honor today. In summation, my mother seemingly lived her life in pursuit of one objective: the well being of her family and every stranger, acquaintance, and friend who was ever blessed to know her.

My earliest memories are from when I must have been about seven years old and my sister four years old. As a young child, my sister would wake up early on Sunday mornings and begin to make the kinds of sounds small children make on Sunday mornings, like blasting the television so as not to miss a word of dialogue in a favorite cartoon. In an effort to allow my father to catch a few more hours of sleep, my mother would get us out of the house and commence what became a Sunday morning ritual.

In short, we'd load into the car in our pajamas and proceed to destination number one: Western Bagel. From what I recall, our standard order was two-dozen bagels, lots of cream cheese, and three coffees. From there, we would drive to Van Nuys Airport and park directly on the runway to watch airplanes take off, listening to oldies on K-Earth 101 and enjoying what seemed like an endless supply of bagels and cream cheese, with my mom's version of a child's coffee, comprised of about seven ounces of coffee creamer, lots of sugar, and just enough coffee to make the drink warm. I know that this might strike some of you as an odd way to spend your Sunday mornings, but it was an adventure my sister and I relished for years.

As my sister and I grew older, our trips to Van Nuys Airport took place with less frequency, and I came to truly recognize my mother's ambition: "my family." It was quite simple; she only wanted the best for us. And when I say that she wanted the best for us, I am not suggesting that we went from watching airplanes take off at Van Nuys Airport to studying for the LSAT, MCAT, GRE, or what have you…she cared about one thing, and absolutely nothing in the world came before it: she lived for us to be happy and achieve whatever goals would make us happy. With that said, allow me to provide a caveat so as not to mischaracterize my mother; her goal to ensure our happiness never involved stepping on other people's feet, like asking my basketball coach why I was a benchwarmer or telling my middle-school Spanish teacher that I deserved a higher grade. For lack of a better way of putting it, my mother dedicated her life to my family in a beautiful way, providing me with a best friend, confidant, and mother whose life was taken prematurely.

In the spirit of brevity, I would like you to imagine the times that my mother happily lent you her hand. There's no reason for me to go into details on this point because if you knew my mother, you'll likely remember that she happily wanted to do anything she could for you with no expectation of anything in return. Insofar as we can try to implement only a fraction of the beauty that my mom brought into this world, her spirit will not only rest in heaven, but her sparks will remain right here on the earth and make the quality of each of our days that much better.

With the loss of my mother, I am disheartened, angry, devastated, outraged, and sickened from my bones to my soul. However, the sparks from heaven that I believe my mother brought down to this world continue to sparkle in my life and hopefully each of your lives. Thank you all for being a part of my mother's life and, again, thank you for taking the time to celebrate her life on this very difficult day.

About one thousand people attended the funeral. Someone attending another funeral asked what celebrity was being buried at Memorial Park. Far from a celebrity, Joanne was a humble, gentle woman who taught third grade, touching the minds and hearts of her family, friends, students, and every soul she encountered.

It was now my turn to deliver a eulogy. As I nervously approached the lectern and steadied myself before the microphone, I knew that a thousand people were looking through me. I looked into a sea of faces, a mosaic that reflected Joanne's life: the faces of her family, friends, colleagues, students both past and present, and the parents of her students.

It was now time to forego studying the mosaic and share a few words about the woman I loved.

MY EULOGY FOR JOANNE
I fell in love with Joanne when I first met her forty years ago. Who wouldn't? She was beautiful and kind, a rare combination.

Living with Joanne was never boring. I remember shortly after we were married she invited a teacher colleague for dinner. The dinner guest soon dined with us every night for the next year. Joanne also did her laundry—after all, her apartment building didn't have a washer or dryer. Over the years there were countless individuals who passed through our doors. Their stories were similar: they were alone in the world or going through a life crisis. It was clear that I had married a woman whose mission in life was to comfort souls in crisis. On one occasion, Joanne revealed to me that she had just written a check from our bank account to help someone pay their mortgage. She looked at me with those big, innocent brown eyes and said, "After all, Neil, they have two small kids, just like us." I responded that I appreciate her kindness, "but, next time, make sure you don't overdraw the bank account." I was truly married to the Jewish Mother Teresa.

She was my soul mate, lover, best friend, and teacher. The Joanne years were the best years of my life, and at this moment I feel lost without her.

There is a book by Andre Schwarz-Bart called The Last of the Just. *In the book he discusses the mystery of the Lamid Vavniks.*

Who are the Lamid Vavniks? In Jewish folklore, it is told that each generation has thirty-six righteous people, who bear upon their shoulders the burden of all our pain, and sorrows.. On Saturday, April 2, 2011, I lost my soul mate, our children lost an incredible mother, and the world lost a Lamid Vavnik.

The New Caregiver

How could I step into Joanne's shoes? How could I give Amy the love that only a mother can share with a daughter? How could I comfort her? How could I give her strength? How could I give her hope? Digging deep inside of myself, I had to find something transformational, perhaps some residual sparks left behind by Joanne.

April 29, 2011: Normal patterns have shattered like a broken glass. Uncertainty is the direction of the wind. I reach out to grasp a sense of normalcy, but it evades me.

That night, Amy was sleeping at St. John's Hospital in Santa Monica, not far from the Hotel Casa del Mar, where this summer she was to be married. So much has changed so fast in the last year. The nurse was setting up a pain pump. The pain was more than physiological; it now inhabited places pain pumps couldn't reach.

Our current brushfire began to burn on Tuesday, April 26, 2011, just three days earlier on "Chemo Tuesday," as we called it. The intensity of pain experienced by Amy in her spine and abdomen continued to worsen. Dr. Brown, her oncologist, examined her and asked Amy about the pain. It was "bad," she said.

Her tumor markers from the previous week continued to escalate. When looking at her marker chart, which was handed to me by the doctor, I wondered, "How much higher could the markers climb? They are already off the charts."

The cancer was growing. Dr. Brown, always calm and collected and never an alarmist, always offered a carrot stick of optimism. But there was no carrot stick today. Nevertheless, as I looked into his eyes, it was apparent that he knew the direction of this journey. "Well," he said, "I don't think that the Gensar is getting the job done. We're going to have to switch to another chemo drug, 5FU. This drug is directed at the gastrointestinal tract and liver, but it will also benefit the lung. Let's give it a try. The only downside is the delivery system used for the drug. It's a little different. Amy, you will receive an infusion once every two weeks administered in our office for a couple of hours. The pump will then be attached to the port in your chest and dispensed continuously for forty-eight hours after you leave the office."

Amy wasn't happy to hear about another pump. Nevertheless, if that was what it took to stop the invading cancer forces, we had to move forward. Due to Amy's pronounced abdominal pain and inability to hold food down, Dr. Brown referred us to a gastroenterologist located across the street. He was able to squeeze us in as his last appointment of the day. The gastroenterologist ordered an endoscopic procedure for Wednesday morning, April

27, 2011. By the time we left the gastroenterologist's office, it was 5:30 p.m. We finished our all-day medical adventure just in time to jump on the 405 Freeway back to the San Fernando Valley in the heart of rush-hour traffic.

Later that night, Amy had an emotional meltdown as nausea swept her GI tract, forcing her repeatedly to the bathroom. "I want my mom!" she screamed. We were up most of the night. We were helpless and lost.

On April 28, 2011, we reported to a surgical outpatient center for an endoscopic procedure. The procedure was quick. We received the results right away, and they were reasonably good. We were told that there was no tumor in the GI tract, nor was there an ulcer. The doctor said that the GI system wasn't properly digesting Amy's food. There was an inability to break it down. The etiology of the problem was uncertain. There was nothing more he could tell us. Once again, I thought, as I looked at the doctor in his surgical gown, *We really didn't need a physician to perform an endoscopic procedure to tell us that Amy's GI system wasn't breaking down the food she consumed.* We already knew that. The question was why? We left the procedure with no answer.

It was midmorning when we finished at the outpatient surgical center. Amy asked if we could go to the Beverly Fairfax District of Los Angeles to see the wig lady she had purchased her wigs from. Amy had her wigs with her and wanted to have them washed and dried. It was a twenty-minute drive, short for Los Angeles standards.

I approached a small house on a tree-lined street where several young Orthodox Jewish women congregated in the front. They wore long dresses with sleeves fully covering their arms. Their shaven heads were covered by wigs. I parked in front of the driveway of the house, and Amy exited the car. The young Orthodox women stared at her, a slim, non-Orthodox, jean-clad woman wearing a wig and carrying another one. Amy entered the house, and, five minutes later, out walked the same Amy but now sporting short, cropped hair, a byproduct of her chemotherapy.

As she entered the car, I asked, "What are we going to do for lunch? It's lunchtime." "Fred Segal's," she suggested. "Let's go to Fred Segal's. I like their frozen watermelon juice. I have no appetite for anything more." As we pulled into Fred Segal's parking lot, Amy told me she was too weak to get out of the car. She remained in the car while I sprinted to the juice bar. As I waited in line, I observed tables of relaxed, smiling faces, people chatting it up and leisurely passing the time away. It wasn't long ago that I, too, lived a normal life, a life I took for granted.

That night the nausea increased, accompanied by another meltdown with the resonating cry of, "I don't want to live anymore." Fortunately, she had a psychiatric appointment set for Friday, April 29, 2011. As for the nausea, she was scheduled to return to Dr. Brown, her oncologist, in the morning to remove the chemo pump. Wednesday was a long night of vomiting and crying, enough to dehydrate anyone.

Upon arriving at Dr. Brown's office on Thursday and after her examination, it was determined that she was seriously dehydrated, leading to her admission to St. John's Hospital in Santa Monica. After her admission to the hospital, Monique stayed with Amy as I drove back to the San Fernando Valley to pick up Amy's phone charger, sweats, iPad, and a long list of other items. On the long ride back from Northridge to the St. John's Hospital in Santa Monica, I had plenty of time to think. It is times like this that you begin to examine your life in between intervals of chaos. You search for answers, you search for meaning, and you search for the tranquility in life, yet they remain elusive.

Amy remained hospitalized on Friday, though she had a scheduled psychiatric appointment with Dr. Griffin in Santa Monica. Amy had developed anxiety issues while in college. She started seeing Dr. Griffin at that time and remained her patient for several years. Like that of many psychiatrists, Dr. Griffin's role was that of a bartender, mixing psychotropic cocktails and occasionally tweaking the recipe contingent upon mental status. Psychotherapy wasn't part of her job description.

When Amy was first diagnosed with cancer, she started therapy with a former oncology nurse who became a marriage-and-family counselor, who purportedly specialized in psychological counseling for cancer patients. Joanne participated in a session and was less than impressed. She told me that Amy liked the counselor. Joanne wasn't certain why, but we rationalized that it was a third person that she could express her feelings to. After Joanne's unexpected passing, Amy returned to the therapist. She told me that she needed to see her because Joanne and Amy saw her in conjugal therapy. "There was a connection," Amy said. I refrained from telling her Joanne's true impression of the therapist. As it turned out, I didn't have to say anything. After the most recent session with the therapist, Amy felt the same.

Dr. Brown had a psychologist who saw patients in his office. His name was Dr. Scheinbaum, a soft-spoken, middle-aged, modern Orthodox gentleman. He wore a small *kipah* (head covering worn by Orthodox Jews), and he was clean shaven. He looked like and had the demeanor of a physician. Actually, Amy and Joanne had one session with him about a month before Joanne died. The psychologist concluded that they probably didn't need his services because they enjoyed such a close reciprocal support system and friendship with each other. However, Dr. Scheinbaum said, "If you ever need my services in the future, don't hesitate to call me." About a month after the session, we were once again broadsided by fate with the unexpected and sudden passing of Joanne. This tragedy severed Amy from her primary source of strength, her best friend, her mother.

Amy was now emotionally pummeled. I suggested that we return to Dr. Scheinbaum. She agreed, if I would go with her. "Of course I will." As for Dr. Griffin, her longtime psychiatrist, she couldn't see Amy because the doctor was on an extended vacation. Amy booked an appointment upon her return to the office.

Our session with Dr. Scheinbaum went well. Amy and I cried and shared our feelings of love and loss. We received tools to help heal our souls, such as journaling and art therapy. We left feeling a little better, and Amy made an appointment for an individual session the following week. That session was scheduled to occur on April 28, 2011. But on that day, Amy was hospitalized at St. John's Hospital due to dehydration and pain. We called Dr. Griffin, Amy's psychiatrist, to see if she had returned from her trip and would be available to see Amy in the hospital rather than at her office, which was about two blocks from the hospital. Dr. Griffin got on the phone and indicated that she had just returned from a long trip. She told Amy this might be a good opportunity to get a new psychiatrist. "I've decided to change the nature of my practice. I'm sorry to hear about your mother, and I hope that you feel better, too." She added, "I'm sorry about everything. Good-bye." After several years, the psychiatrist-patient relationship ended in sixty seconds.

Dr. Scheinbaum happened to be in Amy's hospital room at the time of the phone call. He suggested maybe there was more than met the eye, and something was going on in the psychiatrist's personal life. Nevertheless, in my opinion, summarily leaving a patient under these dire circumstances to deal with grave emotional trauma was nothing less than deplorable. Dr. Scheinbaum wished us a good *Shabbos* (Sabbath) and said he would make a *mesha bera* for Amy (prayer for good health). Amy's prayers were simply to be released from the hospital. She ended the day hooked up to an IV, still feeling nauseous. Perhaps tomorrow would be a better day.

Saturday, April 30, 2011—Amy said that the nausea was improving, even though it wasn't. She just wanted out of the hospital in the worst way. Hospitals can strip you of your self-esteem, your dignity, and your hope. We knew she had to get out. As the multi medical specialists made their rounds on Saturday, we sensed they knew that Amy was embellishing on how good she now felt and how the nausea was gone. As each doctor paraded in, Amy would look at them with her big brown eyes, short-cropped black hair, and childlike innocence, asking, "Can I go home today, Doctor?"

Dr. Brown's partner was making his rounds that Saturday. He responded to Amy's request to be discharged as follows: "You were dehydrated the last two days. You're just beginning to keep down pureed food and fluids. If you are released and have to be readmitted over the weekend, you will have to go through the ER, and that could take four to twelve hours. Let's hedge on the side of caution and keep you another day. The plan will be to release you tomorrow morning." He then said, "Technically, the hospital protocol is for the hospital internist to release you." Once again, I was totally confused. The doctor told Amy he would release her tomorrow morning but said it was really up to another doctor. The other doctor saw Amy twice in the hospital; neither visit exceeded sixty seconds. Amy's oncologists were her primary-care physicians and the gatekeepers. I've come to the conclusion that there's so much passing the ball in medicine that maybe the doctors should trade in their white coats for basketball jerseys. Anyway, we were stuck in the hospital for at least another night with growing optimism that tomorrow morning would be our day of liberation.

The evening was uneventful. Amy was in better spirits and seemed to be feeling reasonably good. Family and friends spent most of Saturday visiting and comforting her. By the evening, it was again just the two of us. We played some games that we used to play as a family on long road trips, games like geography and trivia. We attempted to pass the time despite our realization that our brain cells weren't working on all cylinders, leading to long pauses and ultimately the end of our games.

By 11:00 p.m., Amy had her hospital bed lowered to a near horizontal position. She immediately fell asleep. I slept on the bench across from her, a hard bench that I was getting used to. Our brief periods of sleep would be interrupted by a parade of healthcare professionals taking blood pressure, temperature readings, oxygen readings, and changing IV bags. Hospitals are no place for rest.

It was approximately 5:00 a.m. The difference between day and night wasn't discernible. With this background of ambiguity, I heard a nurse's voice say, "Okay, the fever is one-hundred-point-five." Had our hopes once again been quashed? The medical team soon began to take blood to rule out infection. The primary source of a possible infection was the port. They also took a urine sample to rule out a bladder infection. Finally, a chest X-ray was taken. The nurse returned at six-thirty for another temperature reading before the changing of shifts. The thermometer was placed under Amy's tongue; the suspense built. "One hundred even," the nurse reported. Amy was given Tylenol. She fell asleep, and I took the elevator to the second floor to get a cup of coffee and prepare myself for another day of uncertainty.

I went to the hospital cafeteria, brought my coffee back to her room, and watched TV. Most stations were covering the stale story of the royal wedding. I guess everyone's life is placed on hold from time to time. Some wait for a government to allocate money for an extraordinary honeymoon while others have simpler aspirations, like being able to sleep in their own beds at home.

Shortly after 9:00 a.m. and after the shift change, the new nurse took Amy's vitals and temperature. "Ninety-eight-point-four," she said, which brought a smile to Amy's face and, of course, to mine. The question remained: would we hear from the doctor discharging her today?

Finally, Amy was released on Sunday afternoon. My brother, Randy, and his wife, Nancy, met us at our home. They brought a juicer to make Amy a banana smoothie. She was on a strict pureed liquid diet. At 2:00 a.m. on Monday morning, Amy spiked a fever. I gave her Extra-Strength Tylenol, which brought the temperature down to normal. She returned to sleep.

On Monday, May 2, we had a ten o'clock appointment with the pain-management doctor in Santa Monica. He gave Amy a shot in the abdomen that he explained was similar to Novocain. "It will numb the pain in your stomach," he said. After we left his office, I asked Amy if she was feeling better.

Her response was, "I'm exactly the same." The shot had done nothing.

◂─●─▸

Sunday May 15, 2011: The pain in the liver was intractable, the nausea constant, dissipating Amy's appetite to fleeting moments when an attempt was made to drink an Ensure or hold down a few sips of chicken noodle soup. The fluid was building up again in her lungs, and her breathing manifested a high-pitched wheeze. How courageous could this slender, beautiful, brown-eyed girl be? Her gait was now altered by a fractured hip caused by the bone cancer, which weakened her musculoskeletal system and affected her spine. Pain patches and pain pills couldn't put out the fire. And so finally her spirit broke.

"Dad, I can't go on any longer. I'm ready to die. I have no quality of life, I'm getting worse each day, and my illness is unbearable. I don't want to live anymore, and I most certainly don't want any more chemotherapy." She cried, and there were no words that I could console her with. A trial lawyer my entire life, a wordsmith by trade, I was now at a loss for words. My vocabulary was an empty well.

Soon the Ativan and pain medication kicked in, and Amy was at peace and asleep.

On Monday, May 16, we had an appointment at seven in the evening with the pain-management doctor in Santa Monica. The waiting room was filled with those afflicted by chronic pain, whether caused by cancer or an orthopedic condition. Their eyes were sunken and their souls lost. If you weren't depressed before you entered the office, you were when you left.

Earlier in the evening when we arrived at the doctor's office, we encountered a massive parking structure that serves both the hospital and medical towers both east and west. The lot was poorly lit. More important, on this evening after exiting the car and taking copious notes as to the floor number we were parked on and the color code and spot, Amy snapped, "Come on, Dad, hurry up. We're already late, and we have a long walk to the elevator." Amy walked slowly and in pain, even though she was in a hurry. Her mind appeared to be walking faster than her feet. She was noticeably short-winded. Upon reaching the elevator, we noticed a sign: "Please go to the front lobby security for entrance." I immediately called the pain-management's doctor's office to say we would be late. The receptionist said, "Didn't anyone ever tell you that after seven o'clock you have to enter the building through the lobby?" I said, "If someone had told me that, I would have been in your office twenty minutes ago."

We eventually made it up to the office and into the examining room, where the doctor greeted us with his usual and customary long needle to inject into Amy's trigger point. This time the trigger point was in the spine. Much to my surprise, Amy sharply and abruptly stated, "Sorry, Doctor, no shot tonight." The doctor, taken aback by the directive, said, "Then why are you here?" Amy said, "I don't know why I'm here." The doctor, amazed, asked, "Are you having pain?" Amy responded, "Yes." He asked, "Is the pain better or worse than it was last week?" "Worse," Amy said. "Then why don't you want an injection?" "Because you give me injections every week. They're painful, and they aren't helping me." *Compelling argument,* I thought. How could you help but not agree with Amy? The doctor sharply rebutted, "Amy, the shots are cumulative, and you'll feel the benefit soon. You have to stick with it." "Okay," she said. "Let's get it over with. Give me the shot." Once again Amy realized no benefit from the injections.

May 17, 2011: The next day, the merry-go-round of doctors continued. It was Chemo Tuesday. But this week was a bye, and if Amy had her way there would be no more Chemo Tuesdays, no more doctors sugarcoating it. Today Amy would confront Dr. Brown and demand answers to the tough questions we previously had been afraid to ask. "Is the chemotherapy working?" she asked. "Is the cancer growing? If the chemo isn't working but just poisoning me, why am I still getting infused? How long do I have to live?" Clearly the doctor wasn't ready for this barrage of questions. "First, let me ask you a few questions," Dr. Brown said. "How is your pain?" "Worse," said Amy. "How is your breathing?" "Worse," said Amy. "You look great," he said in an attempt to deflect the dark cloud consuming the examining room.

"Let me answer your questions. The tumor markers are continuing to escalate. The last CT scan showed that the tumors on the lung, liver, and spine are continuing to grow." At that point, Amy cut the doctor off. "I'm ready to die. I can't continue to take the chemotherapy if it's not helping me. I'm ready to die." Dr. Brown then asked, "How much of this has to do with your mother's death? You used to have such a fighting spirit." "When my mom died, my fighting spirit died," she replied. "I'm suffering, and I don't want to live this way."

"If you stop all treatment, you have one to three months to live. If the treatment we give you doesn't work, you have one to three months to live. Here are your options. If you reach the point where you feel the cancer has captured and destroyed your life, and you're ready to move on, we can discuss home hospice care," he said. "Amy, this is a personal decision. If you want to exhaust further treatment modalities, there is a possibility you can live several years. I've seen miracle cases. I would recommend one more round of the FU chemo. It may be premature to write it off after two rounds. Clinically, we should do a minimum of three rounds and then another CT scan and tumor markers. If there is no improvement, we can move into the clinical trial stage. This is clearly more of a long shot. As for hospice, when and if you travel that road, and it's the right one for many, we will cooperate."

"I have to think about it," Amy said, and so we confirmed our appointment for the following Tuesday.

On Wednesday, Amy told me that she wanted to sleep at Joey's on Thursday night and visit her friends at the Pressman Academy, where she had taught. Amy was no longer driving and asked me to drive her to Joey's home in West Hollywood.

We left immediately and soon we were on our way there.

As we traveled through Laurel Canyon, with its sharp twists and turns, potholes and bumps, Amy said, "Dad, I think I'm going to throw up." "Should I pull over?" I asked. "No, just turn the air conditioning on as high as you can. That works sometimes." Fortunately, it worked.

"Dad, I've reconsidered, and I want to live. I'm not throwing in the towel. I'll do anything it takes to extend my life, even chemotherapy."

The fighter in Amy stepped back into the ring.

Upon arriving at Joey's, I kissed her and watched her frail, shrinking body slowly and painfully walk to the front door. It was there the reason to live dwelled.

The next day, I spoke by phone with Amy in the afternoon. She was upbeat, but it was apparent that the fluid in her lungs was building up again. I could hear the wheezing and shortness of breath through the phone. No complaints, however, on her part. It was apparent that the will to live life to the fullest trumped, for the time being, an unpleasant physical reality.

The next three days were among the best in a long time. After the stay at Joey's, she returned home Monday night. I picked her up from Joey's so that we could attend Chemo Tuesday. It was the third scheduled round of the FU drug. Prior to the chemo, we had the traditional pre-chemo meeting. Dr. Brown entered the examining room, accompanied by his now-customary smile, a big, warm hug for Amy, and a genuine look of compassion and handshake for me. "So, how are we doing today, Amy?" "A little better," she said. "And, by the way, hospice? I've reconsidered it. I want to live. I will try anything and everything, even more chemotherapy." "Great," he responded. "To me the most important thing is your expressing some improvement. That's what we want to see. Let's go forward with round three, and, if tolerated and you continue to hold your own or feel better, let's shoot for a fourth round followed by a CT scan." "That sounds fine, Dr. Brown. Oh! I forgot. My lungs…I seem to be wheezing more." "I was just going to listen to them," he said. He pulled out his stethoscope. "Breathe in; breathe out." After a pause, he said, "Actually your lungs sound a little better. They actually sound clear."

"Doctor, the nausea seems to be getting worse. A couple of weeks ago you mentioned a medical marijuana prescription." "Amy, many patients get relief from nausea through the use of medical marijuana. In your case, because of your lungs, you would ingest the marijuana orally through baked goods like cookies or other products that are available. If you would like, I will give you a prescription before you leave today."

Soon, Amy was seated in the infusion chair, facing a large window projecting a panoramic view of Santa Monica. On a clear day you could see the Pacific Ocean. You could also see the Hotel Casa del Mar. I wondered what Amy thought when she looked at the magnificent view. Did she see the beauty and mystery of the Pacific Ocean or, in the distance, the ballroom of the Hotel Casa del Mar and the dream wedding that would never happen?

We were joined for the next Chemo Tuesday by Angie B., who was the director of Amy's school, and a teaching colleague. They stopped by on their lunch break to visit and deliver get-well cards from Amy's students. Amy declined to look at them. "They will make me cry," she said. She promised to look at them later and told Angie that she hoped to come back to work in September or at least volunteer at the school. "Whatever you want, Amy. Everybody loves you and misses you," Angie said.

Amy had finally found meaning and fulfillment in her life through her work and associations at the Pressman Academy. As a tear ran down her cheek, I sensed that she knew that while she touched many young hearts, countless others would never know the blessing to have *Morah* (Teacher) Amy. After lunch, we bid good-bye to Amy's colleagues. Somehow Chemo Tuesday always ended so as to coincide with rush-hour traffic. We picked up the medical marijuana prescription as we left the office. And so there we were again, engaged in bumper-to-bumper traffic on the 405 Freeway while driving back to Northridge.

The following day it was off to the medical marijuana dispensary. Los Angeles is full of these stores. It is a thriving enterprise. Unfortunately, most of them are located in seedy areas around town. We selected one in a more respectable part of the city. Just prior to entering, we flashed each other a smile and agreed, "This is so weird." But, then again, our lives, too, were now so very weird.

The weirdness continued upon entering the store. We were greeted by a nervous, chubby gentleman in his fifties. He was about five-foot-eleven with salt-and-pepper hair, which he wore in a ponytail. He sported a thick handlebar moustache, sorely in need of trimming. His wire-rim granny glasses appeared to be a holdover pair from the '60s. Notwithstanding the above, he was somewhat officious-looking, clad in a white pharmacist coat. He asked for Amy's prescription and ID and had her sign several documents. He then sternly rendered the caveat that the marijuana was to be used by her only.

We were then introduced to our consultant. He was a nice young man also dressed like a pharmacist. I assume these consultants are long-time pot users and connoisseurs of weed. We briefly told him about Amy's medical condition. He stared at us with a slightly cloudy expression and a big, stoner smile. "Come over here," he said. "I'll show you our product line." We were taken to the rear of the store, where there were display cases and shelves stocked with merchandise. The consultant invited us to have a seat. A number of barstools were situated adjacent to the display cases. As we took our seats, the consultant stood behind the counter and asked, "So is there something in particular you like to smoke? I have almost everything." I looked at Amy, and she looked at me, both of us thinking of the same word: *idiot*. Amy reminded the consultant that she had lung cancer. "Oh, I forgot. Wow, am I an idiot." We nodded our heads in agreement.

"Wow, sorry about that. How about considering some delicious baked marijuana brownies or cookies?" "What else do you have?" asked Amy. "I have lollipops. They tell me they work real good for nausea." And so we purchased some lollipops. After ringing us up, the consultant gave us one more "Beavis and Butthead" chuckle and said, "Next time you come in, you're in our system, and you get ten percent off. Isn't that cool?"

As we exited the store, the gentleman with the ponytail, whom we first encountered, stopped us and asked if Amy found what she was looking for. Amy responded, "Hopefully." He then reminded her not to let anyone else use the marijuana products. "It's the last thing on my mind," she said. "Have a nice day."

Once on the street, I turned to Amy and reiterated what we initially felt: "Weird!" "Totally weird," she responded.

◆━◉⊂━◆

The following day it was back to Joey's but first a visit with Amy's new therapist. She had one previous session with her and felt that she had connected. I spoke to Amy after the second session. Joey was with her, and she kept it brief; however, she sounded good and said the session went fine. We chatted a little, and she told me that she would talk to me in the morning.

After Joey dropped Amy off at home the next day, she called me at the office, crying. "Dad, I feel terrible." "What's wrong?" I said. "My therapist spoke about death and dying yesterday. She didn't know I was in stage four. She didn't know that the cancer had spread to my liver, my pancreas, and my spine. She asked me if it had spread to the brain. I said no. She said, 'You should be ready for that because it's the next place it usually spreads.'"

Chills traveled up and down my spine; outrage and anger filled my heart. *Irresponsible, insensitive,* and *unprofessional* were words ringing in my mind. Amy continued, "The therapist asked if I was considering hospice down the impending road. She proceeded to describe hospice much differently than Dr. Brown did." I thought this so-called marriage-and-family therapist, who had no training in medicine, was acting beyond her expertise and proceeding to instill the fear that we had worked so hard to camouflage. The therapist had graphically described respiratory failure and the physiological end-of-the-life experience. I asked Amy for the therapist's phone number so I could articulate in lawyer-like language, sprinkled with the vernacular of the street, what I thought of her session. Amy refused. She said that she would handle it herself. I spoke with Amy for about an hour, trying to talk to her in an attempt to instill damage control. It was too late; irreparable harm had been inflicted. Fear reigned supreme.

Upon my arrival home, Amy told me that she had called the therapist. She said that the therapist felt terrible, apologized for, and regretted the manner in which she handled things. "I hope you're not going back to this so-called therapist," I said. "Dad, she's a nice lady. She made a mistake."

Saturday, May 28, 2011: Memorial Day weekend, once a time for fun and barbeques, was now remembered as being in the same month as Amy's initial diagnosis of cancer. It had been a long, emotionally laborious, and incomprehensible year. I will never forget the look in the eyes of the pulmonologist who first knew that our lives would never be the same. I'll never forget the courageous response of Amy, and I'll never forget the heartbreak of Joanne. Her life, more so than anyone else's, began to crumble this time last year.

⋅⊱══◉═══⊰⋅

On Saturday afternoon, Amy and I had a wonderful visit from Joanne's colleague and friend Lara Martin, and then Amy was off to Joey's. I drove her into the city. Upon returning, I met up with Monique and several other of Joanne's friends at the Laemmle Theatre. Woody Allen's *Midnight in Paris* was playing. Joanne and I were big Woody Allen fans. I enjoyed the film, as a hopeless romantic, and it brought back memories of love and romance. I felt so blessed that Joanne had been in my life and deeply missed her. I left the theater feeling alone, lost in the darkness of time and in search of my now-fading past.

A few days later, it was back to Chemo Tuesday. We checked in and were escorted to the examining room. I thought I had been in every examining room there. However, there was a painting hanging on a wall in this particular office. It drew my attention, and I knew I had never been there before. The painting was entitled *Bridge across Time.* I was intrigued with both the content and emotion of the picture. I became lost in the imagery. Graphically, the picture depicted a barren desert with a two-lane highway displaying one barely visible vehicle. In the distance were rolling hills. In sharp contrast, superimposed upon the barren desert and totally out of proportion was a red wristwatch. My interpretation was the glaring message of time trumping space, the enigma of whether the car will make it through the desert and reach the distant mountains, where lies the future. The future is a contingency.

Time is something that we can feel in our bones; we see it in youthful appearances, and we see it in aging bodies. We don't understand time, nor can we conquer time. I then turned to Amy and commented how much I enjoyed the picture. She looked at me somewhat sadly and said, "So did Mom, and I don't want to discuss the picture, Dad, okay?"

As we sat in silence, we could hear Dr. Brown in the examining room next door. The patient had a loud voice that beamed through the wall as if powerful speakers were amplifying her words. She spoke with a strong and thick Middle Eastern accent. Every question she had was prefaced by "I read on the Internet, Doctor…" Dr. Brown answered each of her questions, but as the questions progressed, the answers became shorter. Finally, the big one! "Doctor, I know you can't tell me exactly, but on the Internet it says with my kind of cancer I have two years to live. Is that true?" I thought to myself, *How many times a day and how many years has the doctor been confronted with that question, "How long do I have to live?"* Perhaps it is the most important question facing each and every one of us, the response to which will affect the spirit of the listener. Doctors, I imagine, arrive at the best answer to the question, an answer that is generally not etched in stone with definiteness and certainty, much like life itself.

Dr. Brown entered the examining room. He asked Amy about her pain, examined her, and then fielded questions. On the top of Amy's list was, "When am I going to have my next CT scan? I'm not getting any better, and I'm concerned that the chemo isn't working." In a rapid-fire response, Dr. Brown said, "Let's set it for next Monday. I'll have the results before your appointment next Tuesday. If the tumors are growing, we'll stop the chemo and move to a clinical trial drug. Prior to starting the clinical drug, we will place you on a three- to four-week washout period with no chemotherapy."

Next on Amy's list was the meeting with her therapist. She recapitulated the graphic and unpleasant picture painted by the therapist of death and hospice care. She also told the doctor she was told by the therapist that the cancer in her lung would soon spread to her brain. I saw the rage in Dr. Brown's eyes. "Amy," he said, "this is so untrue. We don't know when or if the cancer will spread to the brain. As far as pain goes, we have medication for people who are in end stage that regulates and controls pain. I'm going to call your therapist and enlighten her. Give me her phone number." Amy appeared to be somewhat comforted by the doctor's words and the fact that she would be undergoing a CT scan the next Monday.

CAT Scan Day

June 6, 2011: We didn't have difficulty rising early. After all, soon would be one of the most important appointments of Amy's life. Diagnostic testing would be performed that could determine the longevity of her life and her future course of treatment. A contrast CT scan would likely reveal her fate. Soon we would be at the Imaging Center in Santa Monica, where pictures of the army of tumors raging in her body would be viewed by a radiologist, who would compare the findings with prior scans.

Amy and I listened to the radio while inching our way from Northridge to Santa Monica. We made small talk and tried laughing and avoiding the reality of the moment. I gazed into the eyes of my petite, brown-eyed, beautiful daughter. I saw an image of fright sketched upon her face. I also witnessed an inner strength that appeared to be fueled by a belief that there was a force much greater than our worldly preoccupations, a force from above prepared to guide and protect Amy and ultimately reunite her with her mom.

The CAT scan didn't take long, and we bee-lined over to the pain-management doctor. It was a déjà vu experience. The doctor once again asked Amy about her pain. Amy said, "A little worse." "What hurts you more: your stomach or your back?" Amy said, "They're about the same." Growing impatient, the doctor said, "Which one do you want injected: the stomach or the back?" "I'll take the back; the shot hurts less there." And so another trigger-point injection and another query from Amy to the doctor: "When are these shots going to start working, Doctor?" "Soon," he said. "They're cumulative."

That evening, after a few calls to Joey, she retired early. As for me, the night was still, and I felt so alone. I sat in my bed and turned to the spot where Joanne once slept—the bed we shared for thirty-two years, where we nurtured each other's souls, where we gave each other strength in the eye of adversity, where we laughed, and where we dreamed. I recalled, one late evening after Amy was diagnosed, consoling a grief-ravaged Joanne. We embraced each other. She asked, "What will happen if Amy dies? Our lives will not be worth living." "No matter what happens, Jo, we will always have each other. I need you, Jo, and I love you more than you'll ever know." We fell asleep in each other's arms, my body dampened by her flood of tears.

Tonight the bed was empty. I felt loneliness like I had never felt. I reached out to embrace her, but only the empty darkness of night slipped through my fingers.

Chemo Tuesday

June 7, 2011: As always, a nurse took Amy's vitals and weight. Her pulse was 120. Her weight 102 pounds, down from last week's 104. Blood was drawn for the important blood panel. The friendly nurse who weekly took the blood greeted us warmly. First Amy was the recipient of a big hug and then me. I had never received a hug from the nurse until today. As I looked into her eyes, I sensed she knew the results of the CT scan. I further sensed that she knew a rough journey was about to become even rougher.

Dr. Brown then came into the examining room with the usual warm greeting, albeit more strained than usual. He started out with good news before bad news. As we would shortly learn, the bad news clearly overshadowed the good news, which was minimal.

"The lung tumor has grown," he said. "Your main pulmonary artery on the right is occluded. This is why you're having trouble breathing. How do we fix this problem? There are two approaches. First, we can send you to Dr. Rand, the radiology oncologist, and see if you're a candidate for radiation. The area around the lung can be radiated and hopefully significantly reduce the size of the tumor so as to relieve the compression of the artery. The compression of the artery is causing the blockage of the flow of air. If you're not a candidate for radiation then surgical intervention may be required. The area would be lasered and a stent placed in the artery to keep it open."

"What a choice: radiation or surgery." I knew Amy would opt for the radiation as the lesser of the evils. Dr. Brown said, "Let's see if you're a candidate for radiation. We'll call Dr. Rand to see if he can see you tomorrow or the following day." Before we left Dr. Brown's office, we had an appointment for Thursday with Dr. Rand.

We arrived at Dr. Rand's promptly at 11:00 a.m. on Thursday. The receptionist, a young Latin woman, seemed traumatized to see us. After the terror in her face disappeared, she greeted us warmly. "Hi, Amy," she said. "How are you?"

I recalled that young woman. Amy previously had radiation therapy for her bone cancer at this facility. Joanne would accompany her, and sometimes they would bring Monique's lap dog, Carlos. Carlos was an eye-catcher and crowd-pleaser, an absolutely loveable little snow-white fluffy dog. Even I, not a lover of the canine world, was crazy about Carlos. Monique would loan her dog to Amy occasionally to cheer her up. And indeed it worked. The office staff at Dr. Rand's also loved to see Carlos. Amy finished her radiation regimen for bone cancer a few weeks before Joanne's passing. She had a re-evaluation with Dr. Rand two weeks after Joanne's death. That was my first trip to this office and the first since Joanne's death.

The first time I was there, this same receptionist was thrilled to see Amy but also somewhat perplexed, looking at me with an expression on her face as if to think, *Who is he? Where is her mother? Where is Carlos?* And then it was verbalized. "Where's Carlos?" she had asked. There was silence. Amy became awkward and didn't answer. As if life hadn't been bad enough a few weeks before, a pack of coyotes appeared early one morning in the backyard at Monique's hillside home. Carlos was outside for a brief constitutional. It was the end of Carlos. Amy blurted out, "He's dead, and a pack of coyotes got him." The receptionist looked horrified. Upon gaining her composure, she smiled and asked Amy, "Where is your mother?" Amy looked down, paused then responded, "She died" and then turned away. "I'm sorry," said the receptionist. I tried to break the tension in the room by introducing myself to the receptionist–it didn't work.

So it was no wonder that, upon seeing us at this next appointment, the receptionist refrained from asking questions. Imbalance and tension pervaded the waiting room. We saw Dr. Rand, and he said, after viewing the scan and the medical chart, that Amy was a good candidate for radiation. Her first session was set for a few days from then.

That night, Amy's pain increased. I asked where it hurt the worst. "Everywhere," she said. "Dad, everywhere." Then came a burst of tears. I sat helpless, sickened by her agony. I went to put my arm around her, and she pushed me away as she cried out, "I want Mom, I want Mom." We both wanted Mom. We both longed to turn back the hand of time to when our lives were so different, where normalcy was boring and taken for granted.

The next day, Amy's breathing was growing noticeably worse. She called Dr. Brown, who told her that she was breathing with one lung. He suggested she should discuss the problem with Dr. Rand at radiation. He might prescribe Prednisone. Amy previously had problems with Prednisone and didn't welcome the prospect of its use. Prednisone had previously blown her up and made her feel agitated.

By 8:00 p.m., Amy's breathing was terrible. Contemporaneously, she experienced increased intensity of her body pain. Anxiety was now kicking in. She was scared and agitated and lashed out at me. "If Mom were here, she would know exactly what to do. I wouldn't be suffering like this." "You're right," I said. "Mom knew what to do. We both miss her terribly, and we both want her back. But she's not here, Amy. Let's do our best to stay focused and in control." "Get out of my room!" she screamed. "Your words don't help me. You're annoying." I knew it wasn't my Amy speaking. It was the cancer lashing out at me. It was the pain medication spewing anger. I left, but in a few minutes I returned to administer Amy's evening medications, and she fell asleep.

On Saturday, we were blessed to awaken, but the prospect of what lay ahead was painted with grays and blacks. I drove Amy to Joey's house then they proceeded to attend a play that Joey's eleven-year-old niece was performing in. I don't know how she did it, but she went. Amy spent the night at Joey's, and I picked her up the next day. She was beaten down by pain, and there was a noticeable decline in her breathing.

That night was a tough and sleepless one. The pain was so all-encompassing that comfort was unattainable for Amy. Shifting her body to find relief was impossible. The wheezing, shrill sound resonating from her mouth was frightening. I dozed for thirty minutes and then stayed up thirty minutes watching over her to make sure she was still alive. The whole time I kept thinking, *If we can make it through this night and witness the sun rising, there is hope that tomorrow may be the beginning of successful radiation.* You know that your life has sunk to a new low when you are counting the minutes for your daughter to receive radiation.

As scheduled, Amy was ready to undergo her first radiation treatment for her lung on Monday. She moved slowly, crying from the pain raging throughout her body. Prior to attending the radiation therapy treatment, we engaged in what was now becoming a usual and customary event: a drive through In 'N' Out Burger. While Amy had difficulty keeping down solid food, she had recently started eating grilled cheese sandwiches with lettuce and tomato, no onions or sauce, and a vanilla milkshake from In 'N' Out. This was now the staple of her diet. It was the first time she had consumed solid food in a long time. We would drive through In 'N' Out every day, and Amy would thank me with an abundance of appreciation as if we had dined at the Ivy.

Upon arriving for radiation, we waited no more than five minutes before Amy's name was summoned. She slowly walked with the nurse, who accompanied her to the radiation room. Fifteen minutes later she emerged, quite stoic-looking. "Boy, that was fast," I said. "Dad, I didn't have radiation," she responded. Then tears burst from her eyes. "Why?" I asked. "The pain in my back was so bad I couldn't lie still." "Didn't they give you anything for it or give you a pillow to make you more comfortable?" "No," she said. "I have an appointment for tomorrow afternoon to try it again."

We drove home, and Amy broke down in tears. "You don't know the intensity of this pain, Dad. You don't understand it." "No, I don't, Amy, and if there was any way to fix it, you know that I would."

A few hours later, we drove to Santa Monica for pain management. With the escalating pain, she was in dire need of some relief. Unfortunately, up to this point, the pain-management specialist had not been successful. The first order of business was to talk to the pain doctor about tomorrow's radiation therapy. I explained that we needed to ease the pain so Amy could lie on the table for her treatment. He suggested that thirty minutes before the radiation, she take a double dose of breakthrough pain medication, along with an Ativan. "If at the start of the procedure you still have pain then take another pain pill. If in ten minutes your pain has not dissipated, have the radiologist call me." Amy wasn't very optimistic about the plan.

We returned home to Northridge that night with a sense of pessimism. Soon Amy's breathing continued to further deteriorate. It became short and labored, sprinkled with the dissonant resonance of wheezing, sounds that spoke to me in a way that crafted a caveat: "trouble is brewing." Soon Amy was hysterically crying and screaming the pleas that I have grown accustomed to: "Please bring my mother back! Please bring Mom back." We both so desperately needed and wanted Joanne. Unfortunately for poor Amy, she was stuck with a less resourceful, less nurturing me.

"Do something," she said. I stood there for a moment in denial of impending danger, foolishly optimistic that in five minutes this labored breathing episode would pass. It didn't, and I knew it was time to call Dr. Brown. It was now 11:30 p.m. First came the Herculean task of getting through the doctor's answering service. Finally, Dr. Brown returned our call. "You have a couple of choices," he said. "First, if you have any Prednisone in the house, give her thirty milligrams. The other option is if her breathing continues to be labored, you can take her to the emergency room. Unfortunately, you may have to wait several hours to get in, and they don't really know her complicated history. I would try the Prednisone first, and if it doesn't work go to the ER." I reminded the doctor that we had an appointment the following morning at ten. It was Chemo Tuesday. He signed off with, "See you then."

After we hung up with Dr. Brown, we frantically looked throughout the house for Prednisone. Amy last took it several months ago. After mounting frustration and anxiety, we finally found an unexpired bottle. Amy took thirty milligrams. It significantly improved her symptoms and kept us out of the emergency room. Nonetheless, we were up the entire night and arrived at Dr. Brown's appointment an hour and a half early. As we entered the elevator to take the familiar flight to the sixth floor, Amy's wheezing and gasping for air caught everyone's attention. Suffering from their own medical maladies, those in the elevator probably thought to themselves, *My life could be much worse.*

Dr. Brown listened to Amy's lungs and quickly attempted to disguise panic with a calm, confident voice, stating, "Let's hedge on the side of caution and get Amy admitted to St. John's Hospital. We can get her some respiratory therapy, a pain pump, and try to do the radiation for the lung while she's hospitalized." And so, unexpectedly, we made a U-turn back to St. John's Hospital.

The next day, Amy had her first radiation session, pulmonary therapy, a pain pump inserted, and a visit from a pulmonologist. The pulmonologist had snow-white hair. He also had a nice energy about him and spoke in a slow and calming fashion. He explained what her condition was and what he intended to do to help. He then stated, "If anyone has any questions, I don't have any answers." He gave a warm smile and departed.

Monique and her sister, Michele, sat with us in the hospital. Later that evening, we were joined by my brother, Randy, and his wife, Nancy, along with Joey. My sister, Leslie, and brother-in-law, Dan, stopped by later. When Joey left, Scott arrived. The long day ended on a positive note. Our friends and family departed, and Amy and I passed out from exhaustion.

Thursday, June 15, 2011, was day two of radiation, accompanied by hope that it would shrink the lung tumor and open up the occluded pulmonary artery, bringing Amy a better quality of life and renewed spirit.

Amy completed her radiation on Friday and on Saturday was released. The next day, she said, "Dad, I feel like I'm dying." This wasn't just any Sunday; it was our first Father's Day as an incomplete family, our first one without Joanne, who had always made the day special. The rhythm of my life was now different.

Amy was in so much pain, she couldn't get out of bed. Her breathing was starting to once again become laborious. Randy and Nancy brought their kids and brunch. Shortly thereafter, Scott joined us. Amy couldn't get out of bed. She slept most of the day and most of the night. The only thing I remember about that day other than "I think I'm dying" were the words, "I'm sorry I didn't get you anything for Father's Day. I'll have it for you next week." "Amy," I said, "I didn't expect a Father's Day gift. Your smile is the best Father's Day gift I could ever have." I looked at her, memorizing her sweet face, knowing that this was likely my last Father's Day with her.

⋆⇒◉⇐⋆

On Tuesday, we had a brief visit with Dr. Brown, who examined Amy. Based on his clinical exam, he said she was holding her own. He advised us that he would have her lungs scanned next week to see if the radiation was working and whether the pulmonary artery was opening. After that, he would decide if he would administer chemotherapy or use a clinical trial drug. He also said a hospice agency would contact us to discuss their services. He emphasized again that this was interim hospice and not end stage. He also stated that this was "assistance while moving from one bridge to the next." The logic defied me. They sounded the same with different wrapping paper. The implication was not a good one. Anyway, we left the office with Amy thrilled that no blood was drawn and no infusion was necessary.

We had lunch at our new favorite restaurant in Santa Monica, a small French café. For an hour we pretended we were dinning in France. The young waitress was even French. The café was so Parisian. In my mind, I knew that this was the closest the two of us would ever get to Paris together.

The Hospice Representative
Comes Knocking

At about 5:30 p.m. on June 21, 2011, a nervous-looking man rang our front doorbell. He introduced himself as Raymond from the hospice agency. He was sweating so profusely, his white dress shirt had sweat stains, and Amy later commented, "Boy, did that man have bad BO." It was the first day of summer, and the temperature in the San Fernando Valley was 101.

He spent about forty minutes explaining to us what hospice was and the various services that were provided. He asked Amy if she was interested. "I'll have to think about it," she said. "I don't think I want to start right away. I'll think about it." Amy's cell phone went off, and she excused herself. While she was out of the room, the hospice representative, looking uncomfortable, said, "I've been doing this for six months. She's the youngest patient I've seen. It's heartbreaking. She's so cute and in the prime of life." I thought to myself that if he stuck around on this job longer, there would be more young patients, more heartbreak, and there would be questions of "why?"

After the hospice representative departed, I checked my voice mail. There was a message from the oncology radiologist's office. Dr. Brown had contacted them to start five sessions of spinal radiation aimed at stopping the spread of bone cancer. The first treatment would be tomorrow morning. "Nothing like short notice," I said. But with bullet-train speed, the cancer was bulldozing and playing havoc with Amy's body–there was no time to spare.

On Wednesday and Thursday, I took Amy for two sessions of radiation therapy. Her condition had noticeably deteriorated, and both the chronic pain and the labored breathing were getting worse. Her condition was spiraling downward.

⋅⇥●⥺⋅

Saturday night was my niece Emma's bat mitzvah. Both Amy and I were hoping that she would be well enough to attend. I was pessimistic, but Amy was bent on it.

That Thursday, with cautious optimism, Amy set an appointment late in the afternoon to have her eyebrows done. I drove her to a small salon in Sherman Oaks. I assisted her in and told her to call me when she was done and that I would be five minutes away having dinner. She projected that she would be ready in about an hour and would call me then. Amy called in forty-five minutes, and I returned to the salon and parked in front.

Upon seeing my arrival, the owner of the salon came out but no Amy. She asked if I was Amy's father then introduced herself and extended condolences on my wife's passing. She referred to Joanne as one of the sweetest, kindest people she had ever met in her life. Then, teary-eyed, she said, "We are all rooting for Amy, and she's a brave young woman."

Amy then slowly walked out of the salon, her gait like that of an aging woman; as she came closer to me, I could see that she was gasping for breath. She entered the car quietly. With a forced but sweet smile, she bid farewell to the salon owner. Within moments, Amy broke down crying. "What's the matter, Amy?" Tears poured out from her eyes with the engines of emotion revving up; her wheezing was increasing and the volume of her breathing decreasing. "Relax, Amy," I said. "What's wrong?" It took a while to gain her composure as well as her breath. "I tripped in the salon. I felt like a fool. People looked at me like I was pathetic. The poor girl with cancer. That's what they were thinking. What a pity! Dad, I'm growing tired of being the poor girl with cancer stumbling through life, the subject of pity. I'm tired of living like this." The tears flowed. I didn't know what to say, so I just kissed her softly on her forehead. There were now no words, only tears.

Amy spent Friday afternoon with Monique. I joined them at Monique's for dinner, along with our friend Lara Martin and Joey. We had some good laughs. After all, at this juncture, humor might have been the only medicine left in our arsenal. Upon returning home, Amy seemed much worse, with gripping pain and labored breathing. I assisted her with her last dose of multiple medications for the night.

I returned to my bedroom and asked, "Where are you, Joanne? How could you leave me here alone? I need you!" Her soft, soothing voice had been silenced, and the warm glow of her being had gone. I was alone. I turned to the Almighty. Every night I dug deep and asked for my prayers to be answered, only to hear the silence and stillness of the night. Was my Internet connection to heaven down? My separation from Joanne was tormenting my soul. As I retired that evening, my thoughts were scattered, and my heart was shattered.

*She was a Bohemian Princess in the era
of the Hippie
Traveling from Chicago to Tucson and
finally Los Angeles
With many stops along the way
Tomorrow morning means Monterey
Where her onetime lover and soul mate
lies waiting for her among the seals
His long coal-colored hair has thinned,
turning white in direct contrast
To his bleached blue skin
He looks out into the Pacific Ocean
Waiting for a glimpse of her angelic face
The waves come crashing in
The temperature is dropping
It is cold and the sun is leaving on
hiatus
Our bedroom is silent and the moon is
obscured*

Emma's Bat Mitzvah

On Saturday, June 25, 2011, my niece, Emma, celebrated her bat mitzvah on the rooftop of the Beverly Hilton Hotel. A panoramic view of Beverly Hills, a splendid, spiritual ambiance, was the venue for this important life cycle event. And, like the stars in the sky that would soon glitter, Emma shined. I sat next to Scott and his girlfriend and a short-winded yet beautiful Amy, along with Joey.

Emma announced that a portion of her bat mitzvah gift money would be donated to the American Lung Cancer Foundation in honor of her cousin Amy, who was fighting lung cancer. A river of tears poured from the Schwartz family eyes. Soon Amy, Scott, and I stood to recite the *Kaddish* (mourner's prayer) in memory of Joanne. The beauty of the ceremony was stifled by the reality that I was now a widower and that my daughter was putting up a courageous battle against a disease that would soon take her life.

The introspection and spirituality following the service gave way to the cocktail party, where forced conversation and social awkwardness predominated.

Many people chose to avoid me. I couldn't blame them; they were invited to a party, and my profile wasn't promising for those bent upon having a good time. And then there were the armchair philosophers and amateur psychologists. You know the type. They love to share their worldly wisdom with those of us who are suffering and down and out on our luck.

One woman, a friend of my sister's and casual acquaintance of mine, gave me an obligatory hug. She had never hugged me before. "How are you? How are you coping?" she asked. One of my favorite questions asked by people is, "How are you coping?" I've been tempted to be honest and say, "Horribly," but it's not my style. I've coined what I believe is the best response to put everyone at ease: "Just taking it one day at a time. Just taking it one day at a time."

Next, the woman said, "I'm looking at your eyes, Neil, and they are so soft and beautiful. I can tell that you are at peace with yourself." Ha! She was so far from the truth. The next big hurricane about to strike Florida was brewing behind these eyes. *Restrain yourself, Neil. Don't verbalize what you're really thinking and ruin the poor woman's fun. But I sure hope this lady doesn't read cards for a living.* I thanked her and politely sought new geography.

There were several more well-intentioned people who tried to find the right words, words I longed to hear but couldn't find.

By now, Amy was fatigued and in pain. "Dad," she said, "Joey is taking me to his place," which was about ten minutes from the hotel. "Can you pick me up in an hour?" "Sure, Amy, I'll see you in an hour." I kissed her good-bye, and Joey and Amy slowly exited the party.

Scott and I soon found each other watching Emma's video montage, which showed our family in happier days: Joanne's beautiful face and radiant smile, a healthy and beautiful Amy.

Upon leaving the party, I waited for the parking valet to bring my car. When I got into it, I could smell Joanne's perfume. I closed my eyes and imagined her soft skin, her big brown eyes staring at me. This was the customary time for our post-party recap discussion. But the passenger seat was empty. I turned up the volume of my CD, hoping that it would stop the tears and fill the loneliness, but nothing could fill the void.

In ten minutes, I arrived at Joey's with a forced smile on my face, prepared to drive Amy home and search for words to lift both of our spirits. Fortunately, I didn't have to as Amy fell asleep about two minutes after getting in the car. Before she fell asleep, she smiled and said, "I'm so happy that I was able to make it to the bat mitzvah."

The Real Estate Acquisition

Earlier in the week I had scheduled a clandestine rendezvous at the Coffee Bean near my home. I told Amy I was going shopping and would be gone for about an hour. It was Sunday morning around 9:45 a.m. I was really meeting with the cemetery sales representative from Mt. Sinai. When I spoke to him earlier, he said he would like to spare me a trip to the cemetery. He indicated that he also lived in Northridge and would meet me at the Coffee Bean on Sunday morning.

Joanne and I had purchased two burial plots for ourselves several years ago. We never thought of the prospect of having to bury a child. Now a third burial site was needed. The sales representative showed me a picture of the park and placed an "X" on the spot where Joanne was buried. To the right of Joanne was my future home. The spot to the left of her was recently purchased. This was something I didn't plan for. Fortunately, the spot to the right of me was available. Needless to say, over a cup of coffee, an unpleasant yet necessary transaction was consummated, and I purchased the plot.

A few days later, my daughter and I embarked upon another Chemo Tuesday at Dr. Brown's office in Santa Monica. We started with the usual and customary weigh-in. Amy was now down to ninety-eight pounds. Dr. Brown listened to her lungs and said, "They sound okay, about the same as last time." He then said, "We'll see you next week and do a CAT scan in about three weeks. That will give us an idea to see how the radiation is progressing and give it a chance to kick in then we will decide between clinical trial drugs and chemo." That afternoon we were off to our third session of radiation to the spine.

Amy finished up her spinal radiation a couple of days later. However, the pain was now at an all-time high. In particular, her stomach and right rib cage rang out with excruciating pain. I called Dr. Brown late in the afternoon. He said, "If it's not manageable, go to the ER." I indicated that the pain-management doctor had added Celebrex to her medical regimen. He felt an additional anti-inflammatory would help calm the effects of the radiation. Dr. Brown said that the Celebrex could cause stomach problems, but since she only had one dose it was unlikely. Hedging on the side of caution, he counseled us to stop taking the Celebrex and see if the pain eased. "If the pain doesn't improve, maybe it's the cancer," said Dr. Brown. I commented to the doctor that it seemed that she was spiraling downward. He agreed and then said, "Let's talk on Tuesday and hopefully she doesn't have to go to the emergency room during the upcoming Fourth of July weekend."

On Friday, July 1, there was no improvement. The raging San Fernando Valley temperatures, topping over one hundred degrees, did not help Amy's deteriorating respiratory system. Late that night she asked me, "Dad, am I going to die soon?" I thought, *Should I lie? Should I change the channel, or should I try to comfort her with the best answer I can deliver, which is far from the best answer there is?*

"Amy, we know that eventually we all die, some sooner than others, some unexpectedly, some expectedly. I believe in the transmigration of souls. Our body is merely the vessel that transports us through this life. The best plastic surgeons in Beverly Hills can work to make the vessel younger, yet it will still fall vulnerable to the power of time and the elements of the toxic material world. The soul, however, lives forever. Dying is a process leading to an ascent to Gan Eden (Garden of Eden). It is there that the next chapter of our journey begins."

"How do you know that?" Amy asked. "I have to believe that, Amy; we both have to believe that." "Dad," she said, "I think I'm ready for hospice. Will you call them first thing tomorrow?"

Hospice

On Saturday, July 2, 2011, hospice became a reality. It began with a knock on the door. I opened it, and there stood a thin, bespeckled woman with short, cropped hair. "Hi, I'm Maddy, your nurse case manager from hospice." In a nutshell, she was a bundle of energy and a compulsive talker. She told us that when she wasn't working as a hospice nurse, she was a standup comic.

She did the initial intake and described the process of hospice. Amy's breathing and nausea was now at an all-time low point, and her spirit was beaten to the ground. The nurse left at about 6:00 p.m. and said that she would have an oxygen machine and additional nausea medication delivered first thing the next morning. It was a long and painful night for Amy; she looked at me with her big brown eyes, which were now bordered by large, dark circles. "Dad," she said, "I'm dying, aren't I?" I couldn't answer the question. I didn't want to answer the question. I took her hand and squeezed it.

The Long Fourth of July Weekend

This was the first Fourth of July that the Schwartz family wasn't intact. There was no Joanne, and Scott had other plans. It was just Amy and I. As promised, the oxygen machine and medication had been delivered the day before. After Amy was hooked up to the machine, there was a noticeable improvement in her condition. Still, she was too fatigued and short of breath to make any social engagements.

Joanne and I had loved the fresh peach pie at Marie Callendar's; it was seasonal and usually became available a few days before the Fourth of July. So Amy and I drove the familiar route there to get that delicious peach pie that we all loved so much. We brought it home, looked at it, and, both slightly teary-eyed, shared our thoughts at how big the pie was for just the two of us, especially with Amy barely eating. We proceeded to place it in the refrigerator and discussed our dinner plans for the Fourth.

We had been living on takeout food over the last several weeks: In 'N' Out Burger and chicken soup from Brent's Deli. But tonight Amy wanted something special; she wanted to dine out. Most restaurants were closed for the holiday, so we opted for a local Chinese restaurant, a long-time family favorite. As we were seated, instead of the four of us, once again it was just Amy and I. Amy ate more than usual: a small amount of soup, some vegetarian mushu. The waitress kept pouring tea, and we continuously consumed it. We reminisced about better times. Later that night we figured out why we couldn't sleep. We were wired from drinking too much caffeinated tea and were up the entire night. Amy and I actually shared a few laughs looking back out the rearview mirror of the past. She gave me a beautiful smile that I will never forget and said, "Dad, this was a beautiful Fourth of July." *Indeed*, I thought, *one I will cherish forever.*

Weighing In

At the next Chemo Tuesday, Amy weighed in at ninety-four pounds, an all-time low. Dr. Brown examined her and asked about her symptoms. He favorably applauded her decision to be admitted into the hospice program. Amy then looked at him and asked if she was dying. For the first time, there was no sugarcoating. "You do seem to be getting worse and not responding to therapy," he said. "I don't know how long you have, maybe a few weeks or it could be a few years. I don't know. All I know is you're on a dangerous path with the weight loss. If you can't put the weight back on in the next three weeks, the clinical trial drugs and/or chemotherapy that we give you may kill you. It's a serious problem. I'll be out of town for the next week, and you will see my partner, Dr. Getz. When I come back, I want to see a few more pounds added to your frame."

We left Dr. Brown's office and headed for Westwood. Our destination: a nearby local restaurant, Junior's Deli. Amy ordered an omelet, toast, and cheese blintzes, a strong beginning. She actually ate most of the omelet, left the toast, and took one bite of the blintzes. It was an excellent effort for the dwindling Amy. Unfortunately, after lunch, she was very nauseated. Even the marijuana lollipops couldn't bring relief. She went to bed that night depressed, very quiet, and with the prospect of the mystery of death probably occupying her mind.

The Ride to Anywhere

On July 6, her condition and spirits continued to decline. Nonetheless, she emerged from her bed that morning disconnected the oxygen machine and said, in a weak, soft voice, "Dad, Mom used to take me on car rides; it made me feel better. Can you take me on a car ride?" "Sure," I said. "Where did Mom take you?" "I don't know," she said, "Anywhere."

"Anywhere"—a simple word pregnant with so much meaning. I looked at my frail, ninety-four-pound daughter with large dark circles under her big, beautiful brown eyes. Her message was simple, "Dad, take me anywhere." She wanted to be anywhere but here. Maybe we could get lost and find our way back to the simple complacency of our past. "Dad, please take me anywhere." And so for a few hours we drove anywhere. I inserted a CD, and she asked me to turn it off. "I don't feel like music, Dad." I tried to engage her in conversation, but she said, "Dad, I have so little breath that it's hard to talk." And so with no music, no conversation, we just drove and drove, and Amy, deep in thought, looked out the passenger-side window. What she saw, she never told me. What she thought, she never shared with me. But we drove and drove anywhere. To this day I regret that I didn't pursue what she was thinking about.

Upon returning home, I assisted her back into the house, she got into bed, and I reattached the oxygen machine. She smiled at me and asked if we could go on another drive anywhere tomorrow. "Of course! Of course!" I also liked the drive to anywhere.

Amy slept most of the next day. Despite not feeling well when she woke up late in the afternoon, she once again disconnected the oxygen machine and said, "Dad, can you drive me to Joey's?" Ah, a more specific destination. We put her portable oxygen tank in the car and were off and running to Joey's home in West Hollywood, taking the 405 Freeway to Ventura East, off on Laurel Canyon Boulevard, and then taking the winding canyon road into the city. By the time we got to Joey's, Amy said, "I'm so tired, Dad. This will be a very short visit. Why don't you get a cup of coffee and come back in thirty or forty minutes." "Perfect," I said. One of my favorite bookstores, The Bodhi Tree, was five minutes from Joey's home. I hadn't been there in years.

When I entered the store, The Bodhi Tree, unlike most of Los Angeles, looked just as I remembered. The pungent smell of incense permeated the air, mixing with vibrations of the New Age music filling the acoustical space of the store. As for the books, not much had changed. I recalled frequenting the bookstore in the 1970s. I was a spiritual voyager then in search of greater meaning to my life. It wasn't uncommon to make the sojourn to The Bodhi Tree at about 10:00 p.m.. Like a cow in a pasture, I was hungry, and the nourishment I sought was the one book that would unlock the mystery of my existence.

And just as intriguing as the books were the characters of the night that frequented the bookstore. They were people from local ashrams, old hipsters, conservative mainstreamers, and cultists. I studied the faces of these people, wondering who they were and what life they went home to. What answers were they seeking? And, above all, did they know which book possessed the hidden answer?

My mind returned to the here and now, and, after some book browsing and reflections, it was time to pick Amy up. I didn't buy anything, but I enjoyed my brief voyage in what is becoming an endangered species in our country, the bookstore.

After returning to Joey's, I knocked on the door, and he answered and warmly greeted me. He invited me into the den, where we spoke for about five minutes before a worn-out Amy gestured that it was time to go. She slowly got into my car, seeming tired but content. Flashing me a warm smile, she said, "Thanks, Dad. I had a great time tonight." Before we knew it, we were back on windy Laurel Canyon, and Amy was fast asleep.

On Saturday, Amy emerged from her bed in the afternoon, disconnected the oxygen machine, and asked me to drive her anywhere. It felt like we drove endlessly, but it was probably two hours. We had no destination, no plan; I was just seeking greenery, trees, beautiful landscaping, blossoming flowers, and a sabbatical for Amy from her sick bed. We drove anywhere, hoping to find the magical road to our past.

That night Lara Martin joined us, cuddling up in bed with Amy and watching TV. Amy kept shooting smiles over to her and perhaps imagining for a moment that it was Joanne who was lying by her side. Lara left around midnight.

Amy had difficulty sleeping. First it was her breathing then she had pain in the stomach and then pain in the back. We were up until 7:30 a.m., when we both finally passed out from exhaustion.

The next day, Scott came over for dinner along with our friends Joe Penner, Lara Martin, and Lara's parents. Later that night, Scott and Amy had a discussion that I had hoped they would have had years ago. I had been blessed my entire life with an incredible relationship with my brother and sister. I wished that Scott and Amy would have the same bond. When they were younger, they did, but as they grew older, differences separated them. Whether one could attribute it to sibling rivalry or disparate personalities, they were once close, but distance had cut a gap in their relationship.

The encounter began with Scott hesitantly entering Amy's bedroom. She was attached to an oxygen machine. Her breathing was noticeably labored; she wheezed rhythmically and repetitiously. Still, all you could see in that bedroom were her big, beautiful brown eyes, which dominated the spatial realm.

As for Scott, he stared, and his eyes began to water. He was profoundly affected by the loss of his mother, and his grief was still like a steak knife cutting away at his heart. To see Amy in her debilitated state further hurt him. "Amy," he said. "Amy, I love you, and I want to apologize for all the years I acted like a *schmuck*, all the years I failed to listen to your kindly advice and wisdom and responded with anger and arrogance. I love you more than anything and want you to forgive me. This isn't fair what's happening to you. It isn't fair; you shouldn't have to suffer like this. Fuck!" he screamed as an emotional damn broke, and endless tears flowed uncontrollably.

Calmly and lovingly, Amy looked at Scott and said, "I love you more than anything. Please don't be sad." She was trying to comfort him.

"It's not fair!" he screamed. "It's not fair."

In a gentle voice reminiscent of Joanne, Amy said, "Please, Scott, everything will be okay. I love you."

"I have a great idea," he said. "Let's go on a hot-air balloon ride." "A hot-air balloon ride?" Amy responded in amazement while gasping for breath. "Look at me, Scott. I can hardly breathe, I'm hooked up to an oxygen machine, it's a struggle to talk. How can I go on a hot-air balloon ride?"

"There must be a way," he said.

This conversation graphically depicted the differences between Scott and Amy. Amy was sophisticated, conservative, and had proceeded to live her entire life with an abundance of caution. Scott could be the poster boy for the Steppenwolf song "Born to Be Wild," a Harley-Davidson rider living on the edge. They were yin and yang. Nonetheless, as I stood quietly in the corner of the room, I was deeply touched by this moment of reconciliation between my two children, whom I loved so dearly.

◆━◈━◆

Tuesday, July 12, was a busy, jam-packed medical day, starting with a fall. As we were preparing to leave for our appointment with Dr. Brown's partner, Dr. Getz, Amy shouted, "Dad, Dad!" in a weak but frightened voice. "I fell." I rushed into her bedroom. She seemed to be okay. She was sitting on the edge of her bed. She said that while putting her pants on, her legs gave out. Fortunately, she wasn't injured. Nonetheless, it was an overt reminder of her deteriorating and fragile condition.

When we arrived at the doctor's office, it was apparent by the facial expressions of the office staff that Amy's physical condition had changed dramatically in just one week. In the examining room, they immediately brought her oxygen. Dr. Getz, filling in for Dr. Brown, performed a brief clinical exam and asked Amy about the symptoms she was experiencing. He advised us that Dr. Brown would be back from vacation next week to further manage Amy's condition. "If there is an emergency," he said, "feel free to call me."

The previous day I spoke with hospice and was informed that the nurse case manager would be out to see Amy at 1:00 p.m. that afternoon, and the hospice staff doctor would accompany her. They arrived at about the same time. They were distressed to hear about Amy's fall and wrote prescriptions for a walker, a wheelchair, and a shower chair. After hearing her laborious effort to breathe, they ordered more equipment to aid in her breathing. Her condition had hastened downward in the last week with rapid-fire speed, creeping up on us and shaking our inertia.

The hospice doctor was a tall, heavyset black woman with an obvious empathy for her patients. She was easygoing and had a calming bedside manner. While Amy was sitting with the nurse, the doctor said to me, "Your daughter is a very sick girl, and we will do our best to keep her comfortable." The word "comfort" was now being used more prevalently than "hope." For Amy, there was now little comfort and no hope.

Monique joined us that night. She had just returned from Hawaii. She spent the night sleeping in Amy's bed, laughing with her and comforting her. The night before, Joanne's friend Lara had cuddled with Amy until late in the evening. I look at the unconditional love given by these two extraordinary women, and I am reminded that there is remarkable kindness and goodness that comes to the surface in the most troubled times.

The next day, Dr. Michael and Janice visited us. As you may recall, Michael was a cancer survivor who defied the odds and outlived the statistics and had been a source of strength and guidance for our family. Joanne referred to them as her two angels.

Amy's frail body and fading spirit were evident. She warmly smiled when she saw Michael. Her love, admiration, and appreciation for his kindness ran deep in her heart. As their eyes locked, Michael's face revealed the pain evidenced by Amy's deterioration. She was wearing a San Francisco Giants t-shirt. Michael grew up in San Francisco and was a big Giants fan. Attempting to lend some levity to the situation, Michael said, "I didn't know you were a Giants fan." Amy responded with a cute smile and said, "I'm not. You know that I'm a Dodger fan. I wore the t-shirt because I heard you and Janice were coming over."

After Joanne's funeral in April, our sister-in-law Mary, who is married to Joanne's brother, Joel, who lives in Chicago, said she would come out any time to assist me with Amy. She was kind enough to periodically call to check in and renew her offer. She had called me the previous day, and I indicated that it appeared as if Amy's journey was close to an end. Mary made arrangements to fly out to Los Angeles, and I picked her up at the airport on Thursday, July 14. It was a monumental turning point. Amy's condition dramatically changed on that date. Hospice, which had only been providing nursing care for several hours a day, increased to round the clock. Nurses worked eight-hour shifts. A second oxygen machine was added to the equipment in Amy's bedroom.

Among the nurses, the kindest and most interesting was the one we dubbed "the midnight nurse." She worked the midnight to 8:00 a.m. shift. However, she would generally show up at ten-thirty or eleven so that she could review notes from the nurse on the prior shift. She had light-blue eyes that seemed to have a radiating brilliance that looked into your soul. She wore a large cross. The midnight nurse brought calmness to an arena of crisis. As I looked into her eyes, I briefly asked myself, *What is her story? What tragedies has she had in her life? What brought her to this time and place in her journey?* Whatever happened in her past was now transformational. It was apparent that her purpose in life was to bring a ray of light to those drowning in darkness. She explained to me that Amy was in the early stages of transition. This meant that her body was getting ready for death. Her blood pressure was beginning to drop, and her pulse was becoming weaker.

That Friday, I had a private talk with Amy. She told me that she feared death, but what she feared more was the prospect of continued suffering. She looked into my eyes and said, "I miss Mom, and I'm ready to go home." I kissed her on the forehead, and she kissed me back.

That afternoon we received a visit from the hospice rabbi, who was previously the rabbi in residence at the Heschel Day School and a colleague of Joanne's. This was either the young rabbi's first hospice visit or one of his first. What made it more difficult for him was the connection with the family. When he entered Amy's bedroom, his face grew pale. He was speechless. Amy lit up with a smile and said, "How are you, Rabbi?" He responded with a smile. "Good, thank you." Amy asked, "How is your summer?" "Good?" he said. "How are your children?" "Fine," he answered. He then paused and said, "I came here today with the intention of comforting you, but you are comforting me. You are so much like your mother." Amy smiled; she was beaming from ear to ear. She couldn't have received a better compliment.

"Is there anything you'd like to ask of me?" the rabbi asked. Amy thought for a moment and then said, "No, but I do appreciate the visit." He replied, "In that case, I will leave and hope to see you soon."

But the next day, the transition progressed. Her blood pressure continued to drop; her pulse became weaker. Family and close friends began to gather and say their good-byes. Amy was greatly comforted by this outpouring of love.

The nurse on duty that Saturday who worked the 4:00 p.m. to midnight shift was socially awkward. She sported a hairdo much like that of Jimi Hendrix. It looked like she had put her fingers in a light socket. She was very upset with the number of people visiting Amy. At one point during the evening, she asked everyone to leave Amy's bedroom. I asked the nurse to join me in the kitchen. I explained to her that the people who were there were those closest to Amy, the people who meant the most to her, the ones who had given her unconditional love and strength during her journey. As her father, as her primary caregiver and her sole surviving parent, I advised her that those people would remain in the room.

She looked at me in amazement. "You don't understand," she said hysterically, "you don't understand." "What is it that I don't understand?" "There's too much noise, and it's interfering with death. Your friends are creating static, and that static is delaying death." "I beg to differ with you. What I hear isn't static; it's love, and if love is delaying death then Amy isn't ready to move on in her journey. Her friends and family will remain."

Later that evening, in her increasingly weakened state, Amy, with her big brown eyes and sweet smile, lovingly looked into Joey's eyes and said, "I love you so much." She then closed her eyes.

At about 11:00 p.m., the midnight nurse appeared. She reviewed notes then started her shift. At about 1:00 a.m., I spoke to her. I asked her what to expect. She said that Amy was transitioning rapidly. I asked her how long she had to live. She responded, "Not more than twenty-four hours." I wanted Amy to be free from the nightmare existence she had endured for the last fourteen months. But I didn't want to have to lose my baby.

Ultimate Aliyah

Amy died peacefully and with dignity on Sunday afternoon at 12:30 p.m., July 17, 2011. Saddened and numbed, I had now lost my wife and daughter within a three-month time period.

I slowly walked into our family room, where I briefly studied family photographs. I then exited my house, seeking refuge in my backyard, sitting on a wooden bench positioned under a tree. It was peaceful, and it was time to open the flood gates of emotion. I cried in solitude. I cried and cried and cried. There was no way to make sense of what happened. It was still a surreal experience. When would I wake up and return to reality?

The next day, my brother accompanied me as he had often done down life's darkest roads. This time it was to the funeral director at Mount Sinai for the purpose of making arrangements for Amy.

It was on Monday, April 4, 2011, that we had buried Joanne. Rabbi Jerry Cutler officiated. Now, only slightly more than three months later, I once again contacted Rabbi Cutler, this time to officiate at the burial of my daughter. I am not quite sure who was more emotionally moved at the time of the phone call: me, announcing yet another untimely death, or Rabbi Cutler, whose daughter was Amy's age and an elementary school classmate.

It wasn't my intention to deliver a eulogy at Amy's funeral. I discussed this with Scott. He, too, said he was too emotionally drained to deliver one. But sometime after midnight on the day before the funeral, I saw Scott sitting in the dining room with his laptop. I asked him what he was doing. He responded, "Writing my eulogy for Amy." He said that he had reconsidered. I said that I was not emotionally capable of writing one. Scott said, "Dad, you're the pillar of our shrinking family. You set the bar." His challenge inspired me to write a eulogy. We sat side by side until 3:30 a.m., putting our thoughts and feelings into words.

And so on Wednesday, July 20, 2011, the funeral of Amy Beth Schwartz, twenty-seven years old, took place at Mount Sinai Memorial Park in Simi Valley. Before the funeral, I had to identify the corpse. This is a procedure that I had grown too familiar with: first my father, then my mother, then my wife, and finally the most traumatic task of all, the identification of my daughter. As I looked at her lifeless body, I knew my eyes were in contact with nothing more than physical matter. My Amy was now gone, her soul departed to some incomprehensible, distant place where hopefully she will find the peace she deserves.

More than four hundred people attended the funeral. I gave the first eulogy. I spoke of the love and romance between Amy and Joey and how they would have been married that August. I then chronicled the toughest parts of our journey.

I told how Amy was initially given three months to live but courageously battled almost fourteen months until her death. Throughout her struggle, she rarely complained; she embraced each moment and every person she encountered with the love and warmth she had displayed throughout her life.

Upon Joanne's death on April 2, 2011, I assumed the role of Amy's primary caregiver and shepherd, assisting her on the final lap of her journey. The road was dark, perilous, and uncomfortable. I thought I would give her strength, but she was the one who gave me strength. I thought I could be her teacher and bestow wisdom, but she taught me much more than I could have ever taught her.

My life will never be the same, and I will miss her profoundly. She will forever be in my heart.

⋅⋅≒◉≒⋅⋅

Moving eulogies were given by Scott; my brother-in-law, Dan Sackheim; Angie Bass, the director of early childhood Education at Pressman Academy; and some of Amy's colleagues from the TV show "How I Met Your Mother."

But one of the most moving was from her fiancé, Joey, which I share with you below.

Hi, I'm Amy's fiancé, Joey. I am really touched by all of you who showed up to pay your respects today. It's a beautiful tribute to Amy and one that I know would have moved her. Thank you all for coming.

I remember the first day I met Amy in the summer of 2008. It was at work. I guess the somewhat inappropriate part of the story was that I was Amy's boss. She was an assistant working on the production of a TV pilot that my writing partner and I had written. But thanks to then-ABC president Steve McPherson, the project was quickly canceled, thus freeing me up to pursue the beautiful production assistant of whom I had definitely taken note. Thank you, Steve McPherson.

Our first interaction at work was sharing an elevator ride together. Three flights together was all it took. I was immediately smitten. She was so beautiful with these big brown eyes and this radiant smile. And she smelled really, really good, which, if you know me, is like a big thing with me, so that was nice. I remember that day we met was the same day my niece Rae was born. Amy told me congratulations and she asked me, "How do you spell that name Rae? Is it R-A-Y or R-A-E?" I said, "I don't know." And she was immediately charmed.

A couple of weeks later, when we were finished working together, and it was no longer a completely shady thing to do, I invited Amy over for game one of the NBA finals. The Lakers were in the championship, and Amy was always a huge Lakers fan. So I had a small party, invited people over to watch the game. And, honestly, I don't even care about the Lakers. I'm a Sixers fan. But it was all basically just as an excuse to hang out with Amy. So I threw the party, bought food and drinks, and people came. And Amy didn't show up.

And I didn't take the hint. A couple of days later I invited her over again, this time for game number two of the series. I may have even implied, though never explicitly said, that this was going to be a party, too. But when Amy showed up it was just her and me.

And Amy made fun of me for misleading her. And I pretended I didn't know what she was talking about. And maybe the Lakers won or maybe they lost, but I got to kiss her for the first time. And I was so happy. It just felt right, she and I, right from the beginning. And I feel truly blessed to have gotten to be such an important part of Amy's life.

And because it seemed so right, we moved quickly. We adopted a dog, and we named him Rooney, after legendary Pittsburgh Steelers founder Art Rooney—Amy let me have that one—and soon Amy and I had given Rooney a voice, and we would talk to each other all the time in this silly voice, pretending it was Rooney talking to us. He called me "guy," and he called Amy "girl" because he was a dog, and dogs aren't good with names. And he brought us even closer together.

I remember the first time Amy and I told each other "I love you." Or, rather, we sort of did. We were leaving the Grove, where we had driven to separately. I think we had done some shopping, and we were maybe going to go see a movie, but we ran out of time. So we made a plan to see a movie together the next day. Oliver Stone's W, the film about George Bush, was what we were going to see. So, as I got into my car and Amy into hers, I yelled across the parking lot to her, "W!" by way of reminder. And she yelled back, "I love you, too!!" And I said, "No, I said 'W!'" But I did love her. And I think she knew it, even at that point, which is probably why she felt okay yelling it across 3C in the Grove parking lot. And from then on "W" was our little coupley thing we said to each other to say "I love you." Thank you, Oliver Stone.

Amy had many passions. She was an amazing artist and painter, a skilled and dedicated dancer, and from what all the Schwartz's claim, she used to be some kind of soccer phenom, but I don't know about that one. What I do know was that she was someone who always took the best from her experiences and truly savored life. And she loved to share her stories with me. Stories about her family, whom she loved more than anything: her mom, Joanne, and father, Neil, and brother, Scott. Stories from the UCSB days of what sounded like some studying but a lot of partying and making memories with her friends Vanessa and Megan and Jenny. Stories from her fun days working at "How I Met Your Mother" with great friends James and Susie and Dylann. And the stories always had so much passion, and I loved hearing them because I loved learning more about Amy. And I loved the excitement in her voice when she would tell them, and I loved to hear her laugh. But in addition to all the passion and excitement, the stories were filled with many, many, many details. And many, many digressions. Which sometimes made it difficult for me to tell exactly where these stories were headed and when exactly the stories were over. But instead of getting frustrated with me and my poor listening skills, Amy devised a little system. When a story was over, she would finish it by saying, "That's all." And she would laugh because she knew this was ridiculous.

But the thing she liked to tell me stories about most of all was her job as a preschool teacher at Pressman Academy at Temple Beth Am. Amy loved kids. She really had a connection with them, and they loved her. Pressman was her dream job. And I'm so glad that she got to work there for two wonderful years with Angie and Reut and all her wonderful coworkers because I know it made her so happy, and I know, from all the kind words I've heard from Pressman parents, I know how much she meant to them and to their kids. And from all the stories she would tell me about the kids at Pressman, I felt as if I knew them, even though most of them I never met. Those kids were very special to her.

And what makes me really sad is to think about the other kids she will never get to meet. The ones that would have been even more special to her. The ones Amy would tell me in quiet moments, especially recently, how much she had wanted us to have together. How much she had hoped to start a family and build a life together.

Take a moment. Think about one of those family portraits we all have hanging in our homes, the ones of a set of grandparents surrounded by all those they love and created. When someone so young is taken, it is more than just that person who is taken. It's an entire potential family. It's kids and kids of kids. So much life, so much love, so many potential stories snuffed out.

This should've been a wedding speech. It should've been dancing and people holding Amy up on a chair. It should've been smiles and hope. But, of course, it's not a wedding speech. It's sad, and it's tragic. And I'm angry and think this is unfair and all of those things. But I'm also relieved that Amy is no longer suffering. The last year was filled with kind, caring acts from family and friends who made Amy feel loved and as comfortable as could be. Monique and Lara and Janice and Michael and Nancy and many others touched Amy's heart with their devotion and compassion. But for someone who loved life as much as Amy did, not being able to enjoy it the way it should be enjoyed I think was particularly hard for her. So while the last year was hard, I want to celebrate Amy's life. We are all richer for having known her, and she knows we will never, ever forget her.

In the end, I feel lucky. Lucky to have known the Schwartz's. To have known Scott. You got to see every stage of Amy, growing up just down the hall. And I know she loved you very much. To have known Joanne, whom I loved and with whom I'm sure Amy is reunited now. And to have known Neil, whose strength just blows me away. You were everything to Amy, and you've been a hero and, even more importantly a friend, to me. I love you guys and consider myself a part of your family and always will.

And I especially feel blessed to have known Amy. Our time together wasn't long, but it was special, special in a way that nobody is promised, and I recognize that, and I'm glad I got to share the time I did with her.

W, Amy. That's all.

Shivah for Amy

ollowing the funeral, Heschel Day School graciously hosted the *shivah minyan*. There was no way I could accommodate almost three hundred people who attended the *minyan* service that night. The service was just the way Amy would have wanted it: under the stars, a warm but not hot evening. The *minyan* was led by Canter Judy Greenfeld, who beautifully sang with a voice like an angel. Amy's name in Hebrew was Barucha, which means "blessing." Indeed she was a blessing.

On the second night of *shivah*, it was a smaller crowd, perhaps 125 people. The service was led by Rabbi Selah of Temple Ramat Zion. The following night I was joined in my home by a small group of friends and family for Shabbat. On Saturday and Sunday nights, the *minyan* was led by Cantor Avrum Schwartz and Scott. On Sunday evening, Cantor Schwartz passionately spoke about the philosophy and wisdom of Abraham Joshua Heschel and in particular his essay *Death as Homecoming*.

The last night of *shivah* at our home was led by Cantor Judy Greenfeld. Cantor Greenfeld brought a soothing energy, and the service was soulful, with the cantor sprinkling beautiful melodies throughout it.

The *minyans* were comforting, but, with one night left, there was one important piece to the healing process absent. Over a year ago we had received an e-mail from a parent of a child in Amy's class at Pressman. Unfortunately, it was never printed and saved. The night before, I solicited the help of Angie Bass. She seemed to recall the letter and said she would try to track it down. If she found it, she would e-mail it to me. With some last-minute magical maneuvering, the letter was e-mailed to my attention the following day in time for the last *shivah* service.

The letter was from a Pressman parent, Whitney. I asked Rabbi Adam, previously the rabbi in residence at Heschel and the hospice rabbi who paid Amy a visit, to read the special letter. It was dated June 18, 2010, one month after Amy was diagnosed. Rabbi Adam beautifully read:

Dearest Beloved Amy,

We missed you so much these last few weeks and especially these last few days. We've come to learn so much about you since you've been sick. I always feel so special and privileged because you have this amazing, special bond with my daughter. But the more I talk to parents, the more I realize you have this amazing bond with so many kids! Every mom has a special story to tell about you. Every single one of us feels like their child is your favorite. So many moms told me that whenever they see you, you have a cute little story about something wonderful or smart or funny that their child did that day. And I keep thinking, Me, too! The funny thing is hearing all that doesn't make me feel like the bond you have with Lilly is in any way diminished. I'm only more impressed by you.

I knew from the minute I met you that Lilly would adore you. You are smart, cool, pretty, and fun, and all of these qualities completely appeal to my daughter Lilly. This has been her best year yet, and I credit it to you and Francine and Daphne. You are often with these delicate and sensitive little minds and hearts every day, and the impact you have on them is so huge and life-changing for me. You've taught me to see so much about my daughter and her many talents and loves. I am forever grateful for your heart and spirit and sensitivity. You are an amazing teacher and person.

We look forward to seeing your beautiful, smiling face next year. Lilly and I think of you daily. Lilly prayed tonight over her Shabbat candles that Morah Amy feels better soon and said that her candles sparkle like Morah Amy. I agree; they do sparkle like you. With a grateful heart and much love,

Whitney

Amy's response was:

I cannot stop smiling after reading your incredibly sweet and warm words. You sincerely just made my entire year. Lilly's definitely equally adored by me, not to mention all of her friends. I am so flattered and so appreciate the kind note.

The End of *Shivah*

It was the last night of *shivah*, and the crowd began to leave. Soon there were only a handful of people remaining. At about 10:30 p.m., I had a lengthy conversation with Angie Bass, the director of early childhood education at Pressman Academy, Amy's boss, her mentor, and friend. Pressman was so special. It was there that Amy was the happiest I had ever seen her. She loved her colleagues and especially enjoyed working with children. Amy as a child was shy and sensitive. As a teacher, she empathized and gravitated to those students. She shared a philosophy learned from Joanne that education is all about construction, in particular, nurturing and building souls—souls who will one day take their place in society and work to construct a better world.

I had heard a lot about Angie Bass from my daughter. I first met her when she came to visit Amy at chemotherapy. I saw the pain in Angie's eyes as Amy sat in the infusion chair receiving toxic chemicals aimed at possibly extending her life. I also saw within her eyes and her demeanor a mother-like love for my daughter. I now understand why Amy was crazy about Angie. She is a wonderful person. There were other visits with Angie, including a hospital visit. But tonight, the last night of *shivah*, was a different experience. It was an encounter in which we talked about life's most profound topics. We discussed faith, the existence of G-d, and dealing with loss. Angie shared with me that she had lost a brother.

Her husband—like Angie, a warm and friendly person—shared the tragic and sudden loss of his father at a young age. This loss, he said, forever affected his faith. Questions were now raised in regard to G-d, faith, and prayer. I prayed regularly during Amy's illness and someone asked me, "Why bother praying?" I reflected upon the teachings of Reb Shlomo Carlebach, who once said, "Prayer isn't like a soft drink vending machine." People expect a *quid pro quo* relationship with G-d. Put in your one dollar, and get a soft drink; make your prayer, and your request is answered.

Carlebach noted, "In most instances the only time people speak to G-d is when they want something. Is that a relationship that you would want to have with a loved one?" Rabbi Abraham Heschel taught that prayer is not about requests; prayer is a song, and mankind and womankind cannot live without song.

Several of Amy's teaching colleagues were among those who stayed until later in the evening. One young lady was accompanied by her boyfriend. He was tall, thin, and had short brown hair. His face manifested great pain. He, too, appeared to be a mourner. He was quiet and attentive to the conversation about him. He then suddenly addressed me: "I'm sorry, but how can you still believe in G-d after what has happened in your life?" "I gave a lot of thought to that question," I said. "I wish that I could give you a compelling, logical, rationally based explanation as to why I still believe. But I can't. It's something in my soul. It's something that was passed on to me by my father. G-d, like the mystery of life and death, is beyond human understanding. But, yes, even during this stormy part of my journey I have caught a glimpse of G-d through the love and kindness of the supportive community that has held me up and inspired me. And you, my friend, do you believe?" "No, I stopped believing when I was twelve years old, and my father dropped dead at the dinner table after experiencing a heart attack. I never believed again." "I'm sorry," I responded. The lanky young man got up from his chair and left the room.

At the end of the evening, no answers were found, but the late-night discussion was provocative and enriching. Questions were asked that will lead to more questions that will hopefully bring us closer to the elusive answers.

⋅→══◉◖══→⋅

On Tuesday, Pressman sent dinner to our home, and we received visits from several friends. Earlier in the day we concluded the *shivah* as my son, Scott, and I, just before noon, walked a circle reflecting the enigmatic circle of life, a symbolic reminder that eventually we would have to start anew.

The next day, it was time for Scott to move back to his apartment. What was once a home with a vibrant family of four was now but a memory. That night I would start my new life flying solo for the first time in thirty-three years. Just me, the stillness of the night, our dog, Scruffy, and unanswered questions.

Freshly cut years
Taken before their time
Hovering hauntingly in an unmani-
cured corner of
my mind

Packing Up

May 6, 2012: I had just put our house up for sale. I had tried avoiding Amy's bedroom for the last ten months. It was too painful. Last August, with the help of our friend Lara Martin, we gathered all of Amy's clothing and delivered it to a local charity. Her other personal belongings remained undisturbed in her pink bedroom. Ten months later, Scott and I had to finish the job.

There were several journals in Amy's closet. Reading them was painful. Wounds were opened. Scott and I were both brought to tears as we read excerpts from the journals. But, like in her life, there was also an abundance of sweetness. One excerpt entitled "The Gum Girl," written in October of 2005, left a glimpse of her shining soul:

Receiving e-mail was always something that excited me—something that I genuinely looked forward to. Since I became a film major, the sound of "you've got mail" rang out frequently. However, after a while the excitement dissipated into the reality of high-volume information e-mails from the film department or an influx of junk mail trying to sell pornography, get-rich scams, or weight loss. However, in the spring quarter of my freshman year, I stumbled upon what would become my summer internship at MTV's "New Tom Green Show" via a forwarded e-mail to the department from former gaucho Chris Wagner.

I had never applied for an internship, and my résumé was made up of space fillers such as baby-sitting and a long column for activities. I guess I had one attention-getter, my nonspeaking role in The Glass House. Otherwise a pretty unimpressive résumé. When I replied to the e-mail, I expected to maybe gain some interview experience at best—that is if I got a call back at all. Surprisingly, the following morning I received a call from Chris Wagner, and I was on my way to LA for an interview the following weekend. I was interviewed by Chris and the production coordinator, Mike Rubin. The show was barely in preproduction when I visited the Burbank production studio for my interview. Both Mike and Chris conducted the interview in a laidback, friendly style.

The e-mail I had responded to simply said, "Intern wanted for MTV production." At the interview it was revealed that the MTV production was "The New Tom Green Show." At the interview Mike and Chris seemed more interested in talking about UCSB than business. Finally they generally described the tasks of the intern. They said I might be doing anything from picking up phones to picking up Johnny Knoxville from the airport. We finished, and they said, "Okay, we'll call you and let you known if you're selected." I wasn't terribly optimistic; after all, I didn't say much. I just listened and smiled a lot and hoped I would *be selected. A month went by, and I received a call from Mike. He asked when I was going to be done with the quarter. Ironically, I just finished my last final. "When can you start?" he asked. "How about tomorrow?" I responded. "Great," he said. "See you tomorrow morning at nine." I never moved so fast, speedily packing up my dorm and loading my belongings into my white Volvo—destination: my home in Northridge and a taste of the television industry.*

When I arrived at work, the production coordinator, Mike, introduced me to a production assistant and had him give me a tour. The PA was a student at UC Berkeley who had started working at the show a few weeks before I started. He explained that the show was still in preproduction and that there was really not much to do. As a matter of fact, the set for the show still hadn't been built. Quietly, in a barely audible voice, he said that this was a very low-budget production and somewhat disorganized. He sure had a lot of opinions for a kid of about nineteen or twenty who was a PA.

The second week of work, the entire atmosphere changed, and the tempo of the work place changed from still to fast-paced. Since the show was low-budget the producers gave interns and production assistants more responsibility than they normally would assume on a show. This afforded me the opportunity to do things I never imagined I would be doing.

Initially I was assigned to assist the audience coordinators. I worked for the two audience coordinators. The job of audience coordinator is to organize the live audience. I wasn't sure what I was supposed to do but found out the night of the first taping of the show. As the audience checked in and was loaded into the studio, I was told that I had two responsibilities. First, it was my job to escort audience guests to and from the bathroom. I was introduced to the audience by Brian, the head audience coordinator. I was designated as the go-to person if the urge of nature called. Brian then set down the rules of conduct while the show was taped. One of the rules was no gum chewing. He then handed me a large jar. He informed the audience, "Amy will now circulate the jar throughout the audience. Please dispose of your chewing gum in the jar." I was shocked. If I was presented with my job description in advance, I probably would have chosen babysitting. But it was too late. I was now on the road to becoming Amy the Gum Girl.

The show was filmed Monday through Thursday (two tapings on Thursdays). So I quickly learned the most efficient and most sanitary ways to collect gum. Since the only duties I received from Bryan were to be performed ten minutes before filming (collecting gum and escorting audience members to the bathroom), I received permission to assist in other areas.

Since the show was a new, low-budget, late-night cable talk show, it wasn't easy to book "A-list" celebrity talent. The show would often consist of one celebrity-type guest, followed by an animal guest, such as an elephant, or possibly a somewhat random amusing freak (e.g., a space traveler or mad scientist). The audience would often wait outside in the scorching heat for hours while Tom rehearsed with the animals or waited for a celebrity guest to arrive. During this time, I floated the lot to see if anyone needed an extra hand. This resulted in my answering the phones, making phone calls, and running scripts back and forth for last-minute approval before taping.

One hectic Thursday (double taping), I was delivering a script to the set for last-minute approval. I had the script in one hand and a jar armed in my other hand ready for gum collection duty. A writer on the show stopped me and asked what I was doing with the large jar in my hand. I explained that since the audience wasn't allowed to chew gum during the taping of the show, I was entrusted with the awesome responsibility of collecting the audience's gum. Quite frankly, I was surprised he never noticed. Anyway, he found the concept so funny he pitched the idea to Tom and a producer, which led to my on-air participation in a brief segment of the show. I collected the gum and brought it to Tom with the ultimate goal being to build a huge gum ball. The huge gum ball would one day capture the attention of the nation. The show unfortunately wasn't drawing attention, and the gum ball never had time to become huge. The show was cancelled after a brief run, and Amy the Gum Girl was history.

In hindsight, I enjoyed my summer internship despite learning the reality that the entertainment industry isn't as glamorous as it appears. Daily talk show programs are pressure-packed and probably not suited for my laidback personality. Nonetheless, "The New Tom Green Show" was a great experience, and I learned a lot about television production and, yes, the fine art of gum collection.

Who Shall Live and Who Shall Die

As I sat in *shul* (temple) during Yom Kippur services on September 26, 2012, my mind raced, and my emotions were out of sync. Where once sat four, today there were only two. Scott and I sat side by side, a changed and diminished landscape. We were always close but now so much closer.

My mind wandered back to Yom Kippur 2010. And when the prayer was chanted—"Who shall live and who shall die." I thought of Amy and Joanne. I was reminded of the fragile and unpredictable nature of the human condition. The prayer I am referring to is "U-n-sah-ne To-kef." It ends with the words "but repentance, prayer and righteousness avert the severe decree." Intellectually it was difficult for me to reconcile on a rational basis the words of this prayer. Joanne and Amy lived exemplary, righteous lives. Nonetheless, it didn't avert the severe decree.

I found this prayer disturbing and irreconcilable with my theology. In fact, it was so irreconcilable with my theology I felt that I was on the verge of experiencing the imminent collapse of my spiritual foundation. I shared my crisis with a friend. He said that he might have someone who could help me work through it. "I'll call you back in a day or two," he said.

Two days later, my friend called. "Neil, I have great news. Next month the great spiritual master and renowned Kabbalist, Rabbi Rocky Salentar, will be in Los Angeles. I gave him your number, and he will call when he gets to town."

"Thanks. I never heard of the guy. Has he written any books?" "No," replied my friend. "Does he have a *shul*?" "His *shul* is wherever a broken soul needs fixing."

And so about a month later, I received a late-night call. The voice on the other end was hard to hear. Our connection was poor, but we were able to set a meeting at the Coffee Bean and Tea Leaf in Northridge the following day.

Upon arriving at the Coffee Bean, I saw what appeared to be a very large man sporting a black French beret seated alone at an outside table. He had a long, thick gray beard, sunglasses, and wore a gray tweed sport coat with a nicely pressed white sport shirt. His age was difficult to tell, as often it is with Orthodox rabbis. He could have been anywhere from fifty to seventy-five years old.

As I approached him, I asked if he was Rabbi Rocky Salentar. "Yes, I am, my holy brother. And you must be Neil." He then stood up. He was a mountain of a man, probably six-foot-six. *This guy is a Jewish Paul Bunyon*, I thought to myself. While shaking hands with the Reb, I noticed that his posture was very poor, and he seemed to desperately be in need of a chiropractic adjustment to straighten his back out.

"So I hear that this 'who shall live and who shall die' prayer is disturbing you?" "Yes," I replied. "Well, good. It should. That's a normal human response. It should shake you up if you have an ounce of humanity in you. It was the writer's intent to shake you up and make you think. It's what the journey is all about, brother: are you going to live a meaningful and full life before you move on or are you going to look back at your life and say, 'Where did it go?' You must live your life constantly asking yourself the question 'What if tomorrow never comes?' This prayer wasn't written by G-d. This prayer was written by a rabbi. Don't read it literally. This, my brother, is the message of the prayer: In Hebrew the word for repentance is *tshuvah*. The word for prayer is *tefilah*. The word for righteousness is *sedakah*." The Reb then closed his eyes and rhythmically rocked his body back and forth, chanting:

Tshuvah, tefilah, sedakah
Tshuvah, tefilah, sedakah

Soon it was coming out like a mantra. He then said, "Focus upon these three words, and you will see the prayer and life through a different lens. *Tshuvah*," he said, "not only means repentance, but it means to return, also to go inward. *Tshuvah* is to connect with your inner soul. *Tshuvah* is the time to realize that we are all on parallel journeys. Birth is the beginning, life the journey, and death the destination. *Tshuvah* is to examine your life in the context of 'what if tomorrow never comes?' *Tshuvah* is to never take for granted the precious gift of time.

"*Tefilah* is more than prayer; it is song. Music transcends the spoken word and touches the deepest depths of the heart. We must all find the melody that sustains our soul and lights up the universe.

"*Sedakah* means both righteousness and charity. It also means to give. Sometimes we are not in a position to give monetarily. Nonetheless, we are always capable of giving good deeds in the form of kindness and consideration for others. *Sedakah* is a reciprocal synergistic force in which both the beneficiary of *sedakah* and the grantor of *sedakah* feel good. It is an energy exchange on the highest level. Meditate on these three words, Neil, and you will be inscribed in the book of living."

We spoke a little longer, and the Reb said it was time to catch his bus. I offered him a ride, but he said, "Cars don't travel to my destination." I declined to ask for additional commentary and bid him farewell. Watching him slowly walk off with his large body hunched over, I thought once again, *Gee, that guy could really use a chiropractic adjustment.* I also looked over my shoulder for Rod Serling and listened for "The Twilight Zone" theme. As big a target as he was and as slow as he moved, seconds later, he was gone without a trace.

Exit from *Galut*

As I began the exit out of galut, I encountered two elderly women on a dark, isolated highway. They sat upon a bench. They didn't look familiar, but both possessed big, brown, soulful eyes. Emanating from those eyes was a brightness that pierced through my soul. They asked me if I was lost. I responded, "You don't know how lost I am!" "You will continue to be lost as long as you choose to dwell in the past. The past is a fertile ground for *galut*. The past," they said, "should now only serve as a history lesson.

"Remember that which touched your heart and that which broke your heart. Recall your memories, your relationships. The totality of your experiences shall enrich you as you set upon your journey to pick up the pieces of your broken life and build a new life. Recall those who taught you how to love, those who taught you how to be. After pondering your past, divest yourself of preoccupation of dwelling in the past. Move forward, and in doing so you will once again find both renewal of life and love." They then pointed east and said, "Start walking one step at a time, one foot in front of the other. The next chapter of your journey will now be what you choose to make it." They instantaneously vanished. I turned my body to the east and proceeded one step at a time in search of renewal of life and love.

EPILOGUE

⬩⟞⬤⟞⬩

It is January 2013. I sold our home in Northridge and now live in a quiet and peaceful area in Calabasas, adjacent to the Santa Monica Mountains. I am making progress in picking up the pieces of my broken world and rebuilding a new life. But sometimes amid the sound of a stormy winter night, while others are in a deep sleep, I hear the sound of tears falling from heaven. The tears slowly descend to earth and touch my heart. And it is during these private moments that my memory is awakened, recalling how much I loved them and how much I miss them.

There is no quick fix to the grieving process. Recovery is always a work in progress. Some things in life can never be changed. Yet, we can always change ourselves to adapt to the changing winds that occasionally chill our lives. If there is a survival kit to personal crisis, it should contain an antidote of humor, a dream bank, tshuvah, tefilah, sedakah, and, of course, lots of love. As for love, I have been blessed with a new relationship filled with love, joy and laughter. While there are no guarantees about what the next chapter of my life might entail, my past is a reminder to relish and not take for granted the here and now.

⬩⟞⬤⟞⬩

As I began the journey out of galut, my eyes looked to the sky. For over two years my prayers have gone unanswered. Do my prayers lack wings? Has my Creator abandoned me? I dug deep into the depths of my soul, searching for one more prayer emotionally turbocharged with the destination earmarked to the Throne of the Creator:

Today, despite Your silence, I come to You once again and plea that You please answer my prayer. I know that the highest form of prayer is song. But my soul will not yet allow me to sing, so I must find the right words. Bless those who blessed me with kindness and comfort. Take mercy upon and give comfort to those weakened and discouraged by painful afflictions. And for those who think that You are out of business, give them an occasional wink or glimpse of Your greatness.

Please give me the strength to bring illumination to lives darkened by despair and tragedy. Let me find words that will bring strength and encouragement to those who have been capriciously stricken by the hand of fate. Bestow upon me the ability to hold a hand or give a hug when there are no words. Please bless me with the precious gift of time to complete my journey in life so that I may live a life of tefilah, tshuvah, and sedakah, and in doing so my prayer will have been answered.

About the Author

NEIL DAVID SCHWARTZ was born and raised in Los Angeles, California. He is a graduate of the University of Arizona. Neil has been a California trial attorney since 1977. He has been selected by Los Angeles Magazine as one of the "Super Lawyers" of Los Angeles for the years 2008 – 2013. Above all, Neil is a lifelong spiritual seeker.

"An absorbing read, the heartrending memoir portrays the family's tragic but compelling story without sentimentality but with Schwartz's ample love for his family and a wish to help others."
–Kirkus Reviews

NEIL DAVID SCHWARTZ is available for select readings and lectures. To inquire about a possible appearance, please contact the author at neildavid-schwartz@gmail.com.

CPSIA information can be obtained at www.ICGtesting.com
Printed in the USA
LVOW07s1607290914

406383LV00002B/800/P